Best of WordServe Water Cooler / Book 2

OVERACHIEVING YOUR PLATFORM

*95 Ideas to Embrace Your
Inner Sales Marketing Genius*

Compiled and Edited by Greg Johnson

FaithHappenings Publishers

Cover Design: ©2016 Angela Bouma
Book Layout ©2013 BookDesignTemplates.com

Overachieving Your Platform – 1st ed.
ISBN: 978-1-941555-28-6

This book was printed in the United States of America.
To order additional copies of this book, or to inquire about permissions, contact: info@faithhappenings.com

FaithHappenings Publishers,
a division of FaithHappenings.com
7061 S. University Blvd., Suite 307 | Centennial, CO 80122

CONTENTS

III. Before Your Book Publishes: The Planning Stages

VI. Get Out There: Promotional Events

IX. The Bigger Picture

Introduction

Many years ago, a good friend went into a coma after giving birth. She was on life support for nearly four months. We all prayed and wondered if she would pull through to see her baby girl and live a full life.

By her side was her husband. Every day he was at the hospital talking with doctors and nurses, making sure medication was properly being administered, asking questions—basically, being every doctor's worst nightmare when it came to patient care. But you know, on several occasions, he insisted on something that actually saved his wife's life. The third leading cause of death in America is medical care accidents and misdiagnoses. He needed to care for his wife because if he didn't, the worst could happen.

I mention this story because I think it can be illustrative of some of the realities of book publishing today. Sometimes, your book is the one on life support, often from the moment of publication. Standing by are publishers and PR folks who are tasked and paid to keep your book alive. They're busy, they have other patients (authors), and are generally overworked and understaffed.

The point is you cannot leave your book's marketing and PR ONLY in the hands of publishers. They'll do their best (usually), but they're not perfect. And sadly, they have the 80/20 principle that is always screaming at them from the higher-ups. In publishing, it's true: 80 percent of the money goes to 20 percent of the books. It's a reality that won't change, so we have to learn to deal with it.

So what should you do, then, as the author standing by your baby, trying to keep it alive?

You've got to tend to it diligently.

With your publisher: ask questions, say thank you (gift cards and flowers are nice) when they do a job well done, give them ideas, don't mention a problem unless you have a solution, tell them what you'll do to help, keep track of everyone who helps (radio stations, bloggers, author friends). Work WITH them as much as they will let you.

What else can you do?

You're holding the book that will help answer that question. You *must* be an OVERACHIEVER when it comes to book promotion. Enclosed in these pages are nearly a hundred doable, practical, and affordable ideas for you to consider. No, you can't do them all. But go through this book with your highlighter and mark everything you actually *could do*. Then make a plan. What will you do during your first month from publication, second month, third? Write the plan out . . . and then work it.

Publishers, agents, and retailers agree: you're only as good as your last book. So if your last book flops in the marketplace, it may very well indeed be your last book!

Don't let that happen. Stay on guard by your book for the first six months to a year after launch, and you're far more likely to get that second book contract. You may even get a royalty check.

I'm so proud of all of the authors who contributed to this book. They've done the hard work in the trenches and have learned from their successes and failures. All they know they've shared with you.

Happy idea gathering.

Greg Johnson
President, WordServe Literary Agency
Founder & CEO, FaithHappenings.com

I.

Laying the Groundwork:
Author Platform

ONE

Marketing—It's Not Rocket Science

Jennie K. Atkins

Writing isn't rocket science, except for when it comes to my stymied brain.

Yes, I program software systems that run multi-million businesses and some consider me a computer geek. But creating an online presence using Facebook or Twitter, or starting my own blog for marketing purposes, scared me to death! What if I did it wrong? What if I put all this work into it, and no one made a comment? Plus, how does having a blog on gardening bring in possible sales for an inspirational romance novel that had little or nothing to do with gardening? Except, perhaps, for the garden scenes I built into my story world.

I read books on marketing. I looked online and even talked to others who explained it in very simple terms, but I still didn't get it. Or maybe I didn't want to. I've seen the bad side of marketing where authors inundated Facebook and Twitter with post after post, vying for a reader's attention. Although having an online presence is the way marketing works, and yes, you must be visible, I knew that type of strategy wasn't for me.

I wanted a marketing plan that was as subtle as the Energizer bunny. Do you remember those ads? A commercial starts, there is a woman turning on the water preparing to take a bath, bubbles rise from the water's surface. Then out of nowhere comes the Energizer bunny, marching across the screen, beating his drum. From that point on, every commercial aired made the viewer wonder (unconsciously at least) . . . was this going to be a legitimate commercial or an Energizer bunny moment? The marketing scheme was perfect. Other than their original series of commercials, not one dollar was paid to other companies, yet because of the subtle intrusion into the normal commercial venue, you were thinking about their batteries every time a new commercial aired! Even if the company sold soap, tires, or lawn furniture.

So, in my effort to understand the process, I pulled out the big guns . . . my son, who had to market himself to raise funds for his trip to Portugal when he represented the US in the International Six Days Enduro off-road motorcycle event.

I showed him my blog and my FB page. We talked about me joining gardening groups, letting people see my name and my posts. (I'll interject here, my knowledge of FB was v-e-r-y limited.) He showed me how getting my name out there as a reliable source of gardening information would make my name "recognizable."

Another concern I had was I didn't want to be the "dumb" commercial. I refuse to insult the intelligence of my tribe—or would-be tribe in this case. Just doing a blog on miscellaneous information (how I started), or on useless information, may get you some readers, but the key is to pull them in. Give them a reason for wanting to come back. People don't have time to read something that will be of no help to them. Especially when there is a plethora of more useful blogs out there to read.

So what is marketing? It's that sweet spot of taking something you are interested in and sharing it with others. As more people find that you are a valuable resource, your name becomes commonplace to them. Then when you have a product to sell— voila! You make a sale on your name alone. Because of your diligence, you will start with a small group willing to take a chance on you because they've learned to depend on the information you provide. As your name earns recognition, your influence broadens.

For any of you who were baffled by the need for expanding into the world of marketing, as I was, I hope this helped!

TWO

Four Tips to Grow Your Platform

Melissa K. Norris

I don't care what you write, if you want to publish and sell books, you're going to hear the words, "You need to grow your platform." This is true no matter what route you take, traditional publishing or self-publishing.

There are numerous books, articles, websites, and programs, telling you everyone's advice on how to do so. I'm going to tell you now, there's no secret or quick one-time overnight trick. If someone is trying to sell you this, they're probably trying to make a quick dollar. But there are tips and ways you can build a solid platform before, during, and after the book deal that are legit and work.

I'm going to share with you what has worked for me and ways you can do the same.

1. What do you have to offer? None of these tips will work if you don't know what it is you have to offer people in the form of your books, blog posts, articles, podcasts, videos, and interviews. Once you know what it is you have to offer people, you can begin researching who your target audience is and how best to reach them.

2. Where and how will you offer it? You need to have a website that reflects your brand, immediately tells readers how they'll benefit from your site, great content, social media share buttons (you'd be surprised how many sites I visit that don't use these), and a way to capture the emails of visitors so you can stay in contact with them. Other things to offer on your website are podcasts, videos, articles, interviews, e-books, and e-courses. You don't have to do all, but choose the ones that work for you at this time and for your audience.

3. Social media presence. You can moan and groan all you want about social media or you can choose to look at it as a chance to share your message with people who need it and can be helped by it. I guarantee you the latter response will take you farther and benefit not only you, but others. Choose which social media outlets you enjoy and your readers respond to. Don't try to master all of them. You'll go crazy.

Pick two until you feel confident and then analyze where to spend the rest of your time. I use my Facebook page and Pinterest the most frequently. My audience prefers these two sites. Pinterest sends me the most traffic, but I get more reader conversation and interaction on Facebook. Some folks love Twitter, Google+, LinkedIn, or Instagram.

The main thing to remember about social media is to share relevant content with your audience. Everything you share should benefit them in some way or another.

4. Join or create a blogging network or group. Find a group of bloggers (or contact and start your own) who write similar or complementary content to your own. Agree to share each other's content on your social media pages. This gives you great content to share with your readers and gets your work in front of other readers who want what you have to give or say. You can also work with these people to brainstorm new projects or marketing endeavors. This has helped my own platform take off. Plus, I get the added benefit of advice from people who have been there and offer support when needed, because at some point, we all need it.

Finally, here are some of the most helpful books I've read regarding growing your platform and marketing:

Platform by Michael Hyatt

Sell Your Book Like Wildfire by Rob Eager

Pinterest Savvy by Melissa Taylor

THREE

The Cheater's Guide to Building Your Author Platform, Part I

Sue Detweiler

With a glazed look on my face, I obediently handed my phone over to "the expert" sitting beside me. As she looked up my Twitter account, which had an oval egg shape for my picture, I couldn't help feeling intimidated by the task of building an author platform.

I had spent my entire life serving in pastoral ministry. When social media first came on the scene, I was suspect of the enemy's evil intent to use the media to entrap our children.

Now here I was, listening to Michael Hyatt talk about the power and necessity of every author building a platform to launch their book. Much of what he was saying went over my head. Yet as I listened for the still small voice of the Holy Spirit to guide me, I simply heard this word: engage.

As I engaged in the social media platform beginning that day three years ago, I grew from four Twitter followers to over 26,000 followers and from a non-existent Facebook Page to over 78,000 likes. I joined the social conversation and found a whole new world of influence.

Since my first book, *9 Traits of a Life-Giving Mom*, hit #1 on Amazon's Hot New Releases for Christian Women's Issues, I regularly have authors seeking my advice on how to build their own platforms.

Let's Begin at the Beginning

The following ideas are informed by Michael Hyatt's video on Platform Building. You can view the video at www.youtube.com/watch?v=Cs_lGffdboA.[1]

1. Start with a Blog

Begin to build a following. Give people an opportunity to get to know your heart. Use your blog as a spring board to all of your other social media engagement.

If you are an author of a number of books, you are probably your brand. You may write on a number of blogs. A foundational part of your strategy is your own blog where you can share your passion and build a loyal following. I chose to use my own name for my primary blog at SueDetweiler.com.

2. Develop a Social Media Strategy

You are unique. Social media needs to work for you. As you begin to see the power of social media, use these principles as a guide:

Use Time Management Tools

Link Social Media Posts

Strategically Post Throughout the Day

The key to social media is to see it as an ongoing conversation with a friend. You are sharing about all the things that you care about. People who read your tweets will know what you enjoy. Don't be afraid to share your personal story and pictures. Provide your tribe with ongoing helpful resources.

3. Be Real

Don't try to appear to be anyone else than who you truly are. You don't have to be perfect. In fact, one of the ways that people will be drawn to you is when they sense you are transparent.

Don't try to be Barbie or Ken; just be who God made you to be. Let your quirks come through in your social media platform.

Don't be tripped up by your own perfectionism and fail to launch into a new thing. Allow yourself the freedom to try something new. Stoke the fires of your own adventurous spirit.

4. Use Video

Video can be really simple. The technology on your smart phone will allow you to do video in minutes. As an author, you can use the power of video to sell your book—by making a book trailer, for instance, as I did on Fiverr.com. Video doesn't have to cost you a fortune to be effective in telling your story.

I also used simple video introductions of each chapter of my book as an additional resource. At the end of each chapter a simple code invites the readers to watch the video or download a printable of written prayers that enhance each chapter.

5. A Gateway to Traditional Media

As you build your platform as an author, others will become excited about your message and help get the word out about your book. Build relationships with other authors, radio hosts, and television hosts. Two events that I think are helpful to connect authors to traditional media are National Religious Broadcasters (NRB) and The International Christian Retail Show (ICRS). There may be other events that your publisher encourages you to attend to build relationships with the media.

---

[1] Find out much more in Michael's book. Hyatt, Michael. *Platform: Get Noticed in a Noisy World* (Thomas Nelson, 2012).

[2] Learn more from Sue's blog at www.SueDetweiler.com.

The Cheater's Guide to Building Your Author Platform, Part II

Sue Detweiler

As a Mennonite farm girl growing up in Indiana, I learned the Mennonite philosophy of "being the quiet in the land." I was taught that it was important not to stand out or draw attention to myself. I never fit in.

You may not have grown up Mennonite, but likely you have been taught to fit in. In subtle and not so subtle ways you have been told "not to rock the boat." *If you write and market a book that looks like every other book, it won't sell.*

Be a Purple Cow

Seth Godin, lauded as a leading marketing expert, has described what it means to find your "purple cow" and market your message.[1] You can watch his video on the subject at www.youtube.com/watch?v=V82OwyF_vBg.

In today's market with so many books, you will not make a lasting impact with an average book written to average people. Marketing today has changed. We have so many choices.

As Seth Godin explains, as you are marketing your book, you are really marketing you. You are the "brand." So as you determine how to market your message, ask yourself these questions:

1. What is remarkable about you?

What is the 2-3 percent about your message that makes you unique? Rather than aiming at the giant target to make yourself look like every other author/speaker, aim at the bull's-eye of being authentic. What about your message and life makes other people make "remarks"?

When I considered which book to write first, I settled in on the thing that people remarked about me the most: I am the mom of six children. I struggled with this decision to enter into this market. You see, I am not a mommy-blogger. I don't like Pinterest and I don't have ideas for how to have fun play dates with your children.

I am a mom, who never pictured herself being a mom. My firstborn daughter and I were rescued from a burning house when she was only five weeks old. Although we were saved from the fire, she developed colic and screamed for hours at a time. When I finally got her enrolled in Mother's Day Out, she was "kicked" out for biting another baby and drawing blood.

Yet, with all of this struggle of imperfect motherhood, I have six beautiful children. Two of my children are special needs boys adopted from Brazil at ages 12 and 8. Just surviving motherhood is remarkable.

What is remarkable about you and your message? What makes you stand out? Tell your story in such a way that your uniqueness stands out.

2. Are you willing to be vulnerable?

To be a purple cow that stands out from all the white and black cows, you have to be vulnerable. You have to wrestle with the fact that what you are trying to do might not work. You have to overcome all the noise in your head that pushes you to be "normal." The best way to overcome "writer's block" is to find the "sweet spot" of your message.

When I first began writing *9 Traits of a Life-Giving Mom*, I started using other people's lives to tell the story. My editor would read it and say, "I want to hear your story." I was afraid to tell my story. I didn't want to be rejected for my flaws and I saw myself as ordinary.

When I began writing the second draft, I began exposing all my faults. I exposed my internal thoughts about being the worst mom in the world.

That's when I hit my "sweet spot" of my niche. I'm not writing to the moms who feel like they have it all together. I'm writing to the moms that are hanging by their fingernails. I found that every mom in the world *wants to be the best mom in the world for her child, but often she feels like the worst.*

What is the "sweet spot" of your message? Where does your message meet a felt need? That becomes your marketing message.

Find your Tribe of People and they will be begging you for more. When you write, you are writing their thoughts. This is not only true in your book but in every other way that you chose to communicate to get your message out. Such as:

- blog
- podcast
- social media
- radio interviews
- TV interviews

Memorize short segments of your material that makes your message memorable. Capitalize on the felt need of your tribe. Validate their personal situation. Become a friend to walk on the path together.

In the next chapter we are going to talk about being a risk taker. We will also talk about more specific marketing ideas that you can employ right away. This week as you go through your day, be willing to be a "purple cow." Make your message stand out.

---

[1] Godin, Seth. *Purple Cow: Transform Your Business by Being Remarkable* (Portfolio, 2009).

[2] Become a part of Sue Detweiler's Tribe at www.SueDetweiler.com

The Cheater's Guide to Building Your Author Platform, Part III

Sue Detweiler

To be a successful author, you need to think differently. Within your gut, an uncontainable passion burns. Your passion is to change the world.

Steve Jobs was a person who changed the world by promoting Apple products. I am typing this blog on my Mac with my iPhone 6 by my side. In a video available on YouTube, Steve Jobs challenged a company to think differently by asserting that "marketing is about values." You can see the video at www.youtube.com/watch?v=keCwRdbwNQY.

As Jobs says, marketing is about values. In this noisy world, your message is a clarion call of what you stand for. Be clear about who you are and what you are about. Where do you fit in the world? More specifically, where do you fit in your niche?

Rejection is Your Friend

One of our main marketing mistakes is to try to be too general. We fail to touch anyone's life because we are trying to touch everyone's life. We "like to be liked." We don't want to be rejected.

There is already a beat of the drum that your soul marches to. There are others who feel the same way you do. They are your "tribe" and you all march to the beat of a different drum.

Before you find your tribe, you will likely find rejection from people who don't hear what you are hearing or see what you are seeing.

A friend of mine, Tracey Mitchell, wrote *Downside Up*. She wrote this about rejection:

1. Rejection acts as a personal conductor, carefully arranging who and what qualifies for your future.

2. Rejection is a friend who withholds no secrets, exposes all enemies, and closes every wrong door.

3. Rejection is a golden opportunity to better understand God's love, human relationships, and gifts of encouragement that lie within you.[1]

Think differently about rejection. The closed door of rejection to your message prevents you from wasting your precious time with people who *"don't get you."* Smile at rejection as your friend.

I had a friendly conversation with a woman representing a publisher at the National Religious Broadcasters (NRB). I shared with her that my background was pastoral ministry. She then asked what my denomination was. When I said "The Foursquare Church" she quickly said, "I won't be able to publish your future books."

I sincerely thanked her for her honesty and then asked, "Why?" She then said, "Our constituents do not believe in women pastors and they are closed to Pentecostal Denominations."

I was so thankful for her blunt honesty. I knew that this was not a publishing house that I would publish any of my future books with.

Fearless Marketing: Take the Risk and Get the Word Out

Fearlessly market to your tribe. Instead of spending time trying to get people that you already know to be interested in what you are doing, throw your net on the other side of the boat and find those who identify with your voice. Here are a few specific tactics to build your tribe and market your message.

1. Free Giveaway. Write a simple e-book and put it on the front of your website or at the end of your blog. You give it away for "free" when people type in their email address. The secret of the email address is that this person who is on your site may be a tribe member. Follow up with them with future blogs and products. Don't worry about the perfection of your e-book.

2. Building Partnerships. Are you spending time building relationships with others who are influencers? I had the privilege of sharing a meal with Dan Miller and his wife Joanne at a conference. As we built a relationship, Dan asked me to speak at the 48 Days Cruise that he was leading in February 2015. Michael Hyatt and his wife Gail also spoke, as well as other influencers.

You never know where one relationship will lead you. Be intentional about networking. Invest in conferences and events where you will meet and learn from people who are impacting others. The relationships that you build on these type of events can become joint-venture partners in the future.

3. Getting the Message Out. Get outside of the box of being a traditional author who waits to be discovered. You have a message, so develop your message in such a way that you have additional products to offer your tribe. If they already love what you stand for, chances are they will appreciate other teaching and resources that you provide.

A Final Opportunity. We are all learners. When God first spoke to my heart "to engage" in building a platform for the books He was calling me to write, I needed to take baby steps. Wherever you are on your journey as an author, let's connect.

---

[1] Mitchell, Tracey. *Downside Up: Transform Rejection into Your Golden Opportunity* (Thomas Nelson, 2013). Page 15.
[2] For examples of free giveaways go to www.SueDetweiler.com

SIX

What is Branding Anyway?
(Seven Reasons Why You Care)

Janalyn Voigt

Like it or not, you as an author are your brand. As an introvert, I find that fact disconcerting. The trouble with
branding, from a privacy perspective, is that it needs to be honest. I don't know about you, but I'd rather hide out in my office
than bare my soul in public. Do you share my hesitancy? I suspect I'm in good company. How many of us would bother with
branding if marketing realities and/or others in the publishing
industry didn't demand it of us?

Enough said.

And yet, if I approach branding from a reader's perspective,
I become more willing to brand. A reader needs a quick way to
identify what I write. Without it, I could lose a sale. From a negative perspective, it's that simple. But let's look at the positives.

Seven things branding will do for you:

1. Create dedicated readers through the nifty dynamic
called *brand loyalty*. Every writer needs an audience base, a
group of people ready and willing to purchase the next book.
Branding helps you draw and interact with your target readers.

2. Keep you from getting lost in the crowd. With the
ease of e-book and self-publication, these days a plethora of

writers market online. Branding will make you stand out, increasing your discoverability.

3. Control perceptions about you. Whether or not you do so consciously, without even trying you'll establish some sort of brand others judge. It behooves you to manage the perceptions of others about you and your writing.

4. Establish familiarity. Readers need to recognize themselves in you and to feel you share experiences common to them. If you and your website seem foreign, they won't hang around long.

5. Let readers connect with you. Nowadays readers want authors to be available. Branding lets them feel like they know you personally.

6. Help you find your writing niche. Sad as it may seem, not everyone wants to read what you write. People have preferences. Branding draws your specific audience, thus focusing your marketing efforts.

7. Establish reader trust. Consumers buy from those they know, like, and trust.

Developing a focused author brand will make life easier for you on many levels. Given that reality, it becomes much easier to embrace, and even welcome, branding.

What is Branding?

As something of an abstract, the concept of branding generates confusion, suspicion, and even skepticism among writers. But neglected or (worse) inaccurate branding can have a negative impact on a writer's career. And that's a shame because branding isn't that hard to understand.

Simply put, branding is the personality of a line of products or services drawn from your essence and informed by your passions and unique abilities.

I'll illustrate. While in the Oregon town of Newport, I noticed the sides of buildings painted with scenes depicting whales, fishermen, and boats. The fact that Newport is a historic seaport would be true without these murals, but their presence make the air seem a little more salty. Newport brands as a seaport. If it didn't, would it still be a seaport? Yes, but it probably wouldn't be the tourist mecca it is. Imagine those same walls covered in the peeling paint found on buildings in other seaports. Where would a visitor with cash in hand feel most welcome?

Newport draws from what it already is to provide its special brand of tourism.

One more illustration: The folks in the obscure town of Icicle, Washington, adopted a Bavarian theme in keeping with its alpine setting. They changed the town's name, erected chalets, and put Weinerschnitzel on the menu. Droves of tourists now come from around the globe to sample *Little Bavaria,* or Leavenworth as it is now called.

Leavenworth's brand came not from what the town already was, but from what its unique setting allowed it to become.

Key Point: To discover your own brand, ask yourself what you can willingly offer others based on who you already are or can realistically become.

Understanding your brand identity eases the process of developing social networking strategies.

SEVEN

Your Name is Your Brand

Jordyn Redwood

I've been delving a lot into marketing books and I've garnered a few nuggets that I thought would be helpful to those who are beginning to develop their online presence—and maybe change the minds of a few who are already there.

Your name is your brand.

In writing, there's a lot of talk about what your brand is. Put simply, your brand is a promise to your readers. If you write historical novels and then write an edgy supernatural thriller, your historical followers are busy scratching their heads and your new readers are doing the same when they look at your previously published books. Writers who have deviated a lot from their promise usually suffer in sales.

But more important than that is how your readers find you. When they search Twitter and Facebook for your profile, how easy are you making it for them? If your author name is Joe Smith but your Twitter handle is @HotTexasDude3000—how simple are you making it for your potential buyers to discover you and your product. And yes, I did search for that moniker and it seems to be wide open for those who would like to claim it.

Let's focus on Twitter. Your handle should **not** be:

1. Something funny and quirky. Though this may garner a lot of followers, it's probably doing little to build your brand.

21

Especially if you don't write quirky or funny—not that you can't be that way personally. Name first. Image second. Your presence should have a consistent *feel* among your blog, website, etc.

2. <u>A character in your novel or book title</u>. What happens when your publishing house hates that name? They require you to change it. Now it's time spent explaining to all your happy followers that Derek Storm (just love Castle!) is dead. Oh, that's another reason. You as the author decide to kill the main character. Unless you are in a position to have complete control over your books, this is risky.

3. <u>Your blog</u>. Again, your blog should support your brand. Not be the brand. When people Google search, they're going to look for your name first. They may discover your fine blog through your name search but the opposite may not be true. My name gets far more Google hits than my blog name. This is what you want to shoot for.

What if you've done one of these fatal errors? Relax. It can be changed. Why postpone the inevitable? Work to make these changes now. Make your name your brand. Work to have a consistent feel among your social media sites. There's always room for improvement. Even though my Twitter and Facebook profiles are my name, I need to improve the feel so it speaks suspense.

EIGHT

Build Your Platform— Get Yourself Some Gigs

Kathi Lipp

Here is a terrifying sentence: If you want to be a writer, you probably need to be a speaker as well.

Gulp.

I know that most writers would rather hang out a coffee shop or with their cat writing the day away than speak. I know a few writers who would rather stab themselves in the eye with a sharpened yellow #2 pencil than speak. But if you are working on building a platform, speaking is your quickest way of doing that.

Just today, I had a woman from Texas call me up and say, "I'm ready to speak, but I don't know how to launch that part of my business/ministry." Since a good part of each of my work days are spent finding speaking gigs, I thought it would be helpful to share some of my strategies. Here's the first one.

Tip #1: Speak for Free

It is the bane of every speaker's existence. That moment when your event coordinator says, "We don't really have a budget for speakers, but we would love to have you come."

In my opinion, unless you are already booked to capacity, take the gig.

Yes, you are worth more than that, and your time is valuable. However, the best way to get more speaking engagements is by speaking. It is a false economy to sit at home all day creating flyers and making phone calls looking for paid speaking engagements when you have passed up the opportunity to speak for free.

Speaking is your best form of advertisement. When someone is sitting in the audience listening to you, chances are she belongs to at least one or two other groups or organizations that use speakers on a fairly regular basis. Multiply that by the number of people sitting in the audience, and that **is** the best form of marketing.

Recently, a large church asked me to speak for free to a group of over 150 women. At first I was put off because surely they could afford to pay me. I thought better of it and accepted the gig.

From that one engagement, I have had three paid bookings, and another spin-off booking. Plus, I got a great recording from that one engagement.

If you are going to speak for free, make sure you get something out of it besides free advertising:

- I always ask for my expenses to be reimbursed, (food, travel etc). Don't ever let your speaking cost you money.
- Ask your venue if they can record you. Having that recording is essential when you are booking other gigs and they want to hear what you can do.
- Build a great book table so even if you are not getting paid to speak, you can make money by selling your products.
- Ask if the event coordinator will be a reference for you.

Action Plan:

Let the world know you are available. Tell friends, coworkers, and fellow church members that you are open for business and willing to speak no matter the fee

Search out religious, community, and industry groups who are looking for free speakers

Even if it is not a subject that you are an expert on or passionate about, see if there is a way you can make it work for the group. This is especially important if you are fiction author. Your local MOPS group probably isn't going to book you to talk about your latest historical novel, but they might just love your talk on Pursuing Your Passions as you talk about what it took to get published. Or how about a talk on making history come alive to kids? Just figure out how to become a niche expert for any group by bringing in your specific expertise.

NINE

Platform 101 for Regular (Not-Famous) People Like Me

Erin MacPherson

Sometimes I wonder why I didn't decide to be famous when I grew up. Because I'm starting to think that if my face was plastered across magazine covers and my name was on the marquis, I would have a lot easier time getting people to read what I have to say.

But, alas, I decided to be a plain-old, regular gal.

And, while I like my regular life with my regular kids and my regular husband and my regular job, I imagine that authors with big-time names and fancy doctoral degrees have a much easier time building their platform than I do.

You see, I write pregnancy and parenting books. And, while I do have three fabulously adorable kids that give me lots to talk about on the pregnancy and parenting front—I'm not an OB, I'm not a nurse and (shocker) I'm not Jenny McCarthy.

Which means I'm not an "expert." And I'm okay with that. But will my readers be? And, since I'm not, how do I convince my readers (and the world) to read what I have to say?

Here's what I've learned about platform building for regular folk:

1. **Stick to writing what you know.** For some reason, people generally don't like to hear advice from people who don't

know what they're talking about. (Who knew?) So, since I'm not a doctor, I steer clear from giving medical advice, but give everyone the nitty gritty details on what it's like to go to the doctor—something I've done a lot of. You may not have a diploma on your wall—but if your life experiences have given you expertise in something, write about it!

2. **Write what you know in lots of places.** Once you've written what you know, write it in a lot of places. Spread the love and submit articles for magazines, guest post on blogs, start a blog of your own and post user-generated content on websites like Yahoo! Shine. Get your name out there—and before long, people will start regarding you as an "expert."

3. **Keep your blog focused on your area of expertise**. For a long time, I wrote blog posts according to the whim of the day. And I found that my readership shrunk and my posts seemed stale. Why? Because they weren't focused. Based on some advice from my agent, I decided to keep my blog 100 percent focused on pregnancy and parenting—and thus, create a level of expertise for myself through my own blog postings.

4. **Get to know the experts in your area.** I had the most amazing OB read and endorse my book. With his endorsement came the assurance that while my book wasn't written by an OB, the advice in it was medically sound. Likewise, I try to stay well read on the pregnancy and parenting front, so that when I publish material, it comes with the backing of the experts in the field.

5. **Get out there.** If you want to get your name out there, you have to actually get your name out there. That means prying yourself away from your computer (fun as it is to write the day away) and meet people. It can be as simple as going to playgroups/school meetings/ministry events and getting to know

people in your audience and as complicated as setting up speaking engagements around the country. Regardless, if you're not out there talking about your book, no one else is.

TEN

"I Want to Write a Book": Five First Steps For Aspiring Writers

Margot Starbuck

When folks contact me because they want to write a book, especially someone who hasn't been writing, I'm often pessimistic. I want to be able to encourage them, but I know this: an agent or publisher needs to see that a communicator is reaching an audience. So what's a first-time writer to do?

1. WRITE

Write an article. Online magazines usually have writer's guidelines available at their sites. (Also google-able.)

Pitch articles to magazines that are already reaching the audience who will read your book. If you don't know what publications those are, ask among your friends on social media: "Moms, what blogs do you read?" "Business people, what magazines do you read?"

Your pitch to an editor—explaining what you want to write, how it will serve his/her audience, and why you're the best person to write it—needs a hook. No editor will respond well to a pitch from you offering to write on "parenting," but if they might be interested if your hook is, "What I Learned About Parenting During My Time in Prison." Give your pitch a strong hook.

Having a number of articles that appear in print or online communicates to an agent or publisher that you're reaching audiences.

2. SPEAK

Drum up speaking gigs. Ask folks you know to help you find venues where you can share the message you're passionate about. Start by speaking for free to build your resume.

Speaking builds your audience and helps you hone your message.

3. BUILD

Build a website. Do not pass go, do not collect $200. Before you pitch one article or seek one speaking gig, build a simple site to let others know who you are and what you're about. Include experience and endorsements to give editors, agents, organizers, and publishers confidence that you have something to say and that others want to hear it.

A website legitimizes your credibility as a communicator.

4. GROW

Grow your audience. Beyond building your website, be intentional about your online presence. If blogging feels manageable—and it might not!—consider blogging regularly. Guest post on other writers' blogs. Post quotes or memes on social mediate that relate to your message. Don't always be self-promoting, though: share relevant content, from other worthwhile sources, with your followers.

Providing valuable content builds your audience.

5. LEARN

Attend a writer's conference. Even if you've never considered it, the chance to grow in your craft and network with other writers and folks in the publishing industry will serve you well.

Bottom line: If you're not willing to start building with one or more of these building blocks, it's unlikely that an agent or publisher will consider the book you're holding in your heart.

The exception, of course, is if you are: the President of the United States, the MVP of the NBA, or someone whose face has graced the cover of People magazine. If you are any of these, disregard this post. The rest of us, though, need to be hustling to build an audience.

Your future agent or publisher will thank you.

ELEVEN

A New Resource for Your Platform

Greg Johnson

My right pointer finger was getting sore. Why? I had smashed the delete button on my computer to that "not for us" email from another editor on a book proposal they said they wanted, and one I really believed in.

And my thumb had a bruise. I had pressed "end call" on another kind phone rejection for a project everyone had said they were really excited about.

Yelling from my office to my at-the-time assistant Jason, "If I hear, 'the author doesn't have enough Facebook friends' again I'm going to scream. Really?! Mark Zuckerberg is determining what Christian publishers publish now? Is that what this industry has come to?"

It's not that I didn't know social networking results were the first questions out of editor's mouths (yes, before passion, craft, and story). I'd been hearing it for a few years. And my authors were working it! Dozens of authors trying to build their platform with fan pages, Twitter, blogs, guest blogging, guest Tweeting, personal messages, Pinterest posting.

Noise, noise, and more noise.

Yes, it was working for a few superstars who hit the blogging thing at the right moment with the right content. But now there was just the tsunami of words in everyone's inbox. I kept thinking, *Certainly we're getting close to a tipping point where most people are just going to delete everything that comes in.*

I felt bad for my authors; felt bad for the editors and marketing directors who couldn't buy a book anymore just because they loved it. And I felt like something had to be done to help my authors out with their platforms. *Perhaps there is something I could do . . .*

Be Careful What You Wish For

That was in 2013. What once was a staid but exciting "work from home" literary agency has turned into a literary agency AND this nationwide marketing vehicle called www.faithhappenings.com. I now have 454 local websites with national content populated everywhere and local content being slowly added week-by week.

What I hoped would help my authors get the word out on their great books to people who aren't walking into Christian bookstores anymore has turned into something . . . a bit larger.

YOUR COMPLETE, TAILORED, FAITH RESOURCE.

I felt a broadly based Christian website that served people locally would not only help readers bump into books, bloggers, and speakers quite a bit more, but might also make a dent for the Kingdom in ways no website has before. I wanted the site to be able to hold anything and everything—locally and nationally–that was "soul-enriching," "marriage-enriching," "family-enriching," and "church-enriching."

So we launched June 6, 2014, and now have this membership-free-to-everyone national website that has completely automated your ability to find out about:

- Events in your area (concerts, speakers, conferences, fundraisers, author events)

- Products that release from publishers, self-published authors, music, indie music, audiobooks, videos—in 80 different categories.

A new member simply checks boxes if they want to know about when a product or new event is happening, and then they get an email once a week with exactly what they asked for. You never have to miss a new release in your favorite genre again!

Daily Scripture, devotional content (including video), blogs, personality profiles, "resource specials of the day" and much, much more is also included in the site.

If you're an author, speaker or blogger, the site is made for you. You just fill out a quick-and-easy template.

If you want to get the word out on your blog, we can do that.

If you want to speak more in your local area and the areas surrounding you, our site can advertise you as a speaker, and we can also list any and all local speaking events open to the public.

If you have a self-published book and wonder how people will find out about it beyond your social media universe, we can help.

And if you want to offer your product as a special of the day to create awareness about it, we have a daily "Resources of the Day" to help get the word out.

Throw in about two dozen other local and national features and you have a site with the potential to make it so you never have to Google anything local and faith-based again. It will all be there in one website. Your Complete, Tailored, Faith Resource.

So I invite you to go to www.faithhappenings.com, sign up in your local area, and then look around. And if you need assistance, please email info@faithHappenings.com.

II.

Building Your
Social Media Presence

TWELVE

Four Pillars to Build an Effective Social Media Platform

Janalyn Voigt

A social media platform needs a support system, a set of pillars that stabilizes and suspends the infrastructure. Attempting to build a platform before its supports are in place isn't practical or sustainable. Take things logically and in order, and you'll do yourself a tremendous favor.

Four Support Pillars

The first pillar in platform building is that infamous c-word, commitment. Tap into your passion to find the strength of mind and sheer grit to see you through. Decide now to ignore self-doubt and believe in yourself. Determine that *no matter what*, you'll invest your time and talent so you can thrive and survive in the competitive world of publishing.

The second pillar in platform building, self-discipline, is just as difficult and necessary as the first. No one is going to force you to spend time on building a social media platform. If you cut corners, you only cheat yourself. In this book you'll learn ways to work with social media more efficiently, but learning anything new always starts with an investment of time. The good news is that you can tailor your social media platform to fit within your time constraints. But remaining constant is important, and that takes self-discipline.

The third pillar in platform building is developing and adhering to a plan. Thinking through the sites you will use, how often to update them, and who you will interact with helps you make better use of that non-renewable and precious commodity, time. A good rule of thumb is to devote only 20 percent of your time to promotion. Platform building should be a large part of your promotional effort. As an example, 20 percent of a 40-hour work week is the equivalent of an eight-hour day. If you have less hours than that for writing, do the math to find how much time to devote to promotion, and then determine what proportion of that will be spent on platform building. That will look different for a novelist divided between book promotion and platform management than it will for a writer just starting to learn craft. Once you've sorted out how much time to allot, determine how long to work on your social media platform and then follow through.

The fourth pillar in platform building is identifying your support network. As John Donne famously pointed out, no man is an island, sufficient unto himself. Each of us needs the encouragement of others. If you have the support of your family, you are indeed blessed. But even if it takes your family a while to understand your efforts, other writers already do. Seek them out online or locally and support them as they support you. Church is a great place to find prayer warriors who will encourage and pray for you as a writer.

Unless its pillars are strong, a structure can come crashing down. Make sure these four vital pillars are ready and able to serve the platform you plan to build. We've laid the foundation of this series by looking at the spiritual, emotional, and mundane aspects of platform building. In the next post we'll begin analyzing social media sites from a writer's perspective.

THIRTEEN

Build a Social Media Platform: Your Facebook Page

Janalyn Voigt

As the world's largest social networking site, Facebook is an essential plank in most authors' platforms. However, its effectiveness depends on how it is used. Many writers try to use their profiles for business pages, a function they were never designed to support. Even if it were not against Facebook's policies, using a profile for promotion is not effective anyway. There's truth to the idea that friends aren't geared to purchase from friends.

Converting a Profile to a Page

Fortunately, it is possible to convert a profile to a business page with a simple tool Facebook provides. Having recently migrated my Facebook profile to a business page, I offer a detailed perspective on this process in *Convert Your Facebook Profile to a Page (A Step-By-Step Guide)*, available on my site livewritebreathe.com. Would I go back to a profile if I could? No. I've received more engagement and am taken more seriously. As a bonus, I no longer have to deal with unwanted game or event invitations.

Signing up for Facebook and Creating a Page

Signing up for Facebook is a straightforward matter. Instructions for building a page are here: www.facebook.com/business/build. The category that Author or Writer is found under is "Artist, Band or Public Figure," however if you do more than write on a professional level, you may want to choose a different category, like Public Figure (under the same category). If you create your page around your author name rather than one of your book titles, you won't have start all over again building an audience for each new release. Also, leaving out an accompanying description (like author) keeps your options open should you want to add another professional activity (such as speaking) at a future date.

Your Facebook Page

Banner: To promote your brand, its best to post a cover image that resembles your website banner.

Profile Picture: Use a quality image for your profile picture, preferably a headshot.

Tabs: Wildfire, Tabsite and Iwipa are applications that let you install customized tabs to give you among other things a landing page, event manager, contest tab, blog feed, and even fan-gated content you post for subscribers only. Mail Chimp integrations allows you to post a sign-up box for your email list right in a Facebook tab.

Content you post on your page should draw readers who will sign up for your email list. Post updates about your writing progress, appearances, author news, contests, giveaways, and book news. Depending on your brand, you may also want to post snippets from your research, recipes, book reviews, or videos. Whatever you decide, make sure it lines up with your brand and inspires some sort of action (such as entering a contest, signing up for your newsletter, liking a post, or visiting your website). *Make the time you spend posting to Facebook count toward your goals.*

Post Scheduler: It's possible and desirable to schedule posts to publish at a time you specify. This can be a great time-saver. Just click the clock icon below the update window.

EdgeRank: That mysterious algorithm by which Facebook determines how many of your followers see a post is based largely on engagement. One good way to boost your engagement and boost an update's edgerank is to post pictures or videos.

Wall: A page's wall functions just like a profile wall. Like some other pages while posting as your page and those posts will show up in your wall feed, which you can find by clicking the Home tab in the upper right menu.

Engagement: Commenting on other pages is an important way to gain followers for your own. A good strategy is to find other authors with similar readerships and comment on their posts. Provided you don't self-promote and say something sufficiently interesting, some of their followers may become interested in you and follow you back to your page. Doing this actually helps the other author gain edgerank and engagement, and it's possible to share audiences to mutual advantage.

Another way to keep up the engagement on your page is to post consistently. Also, your followers will notice your absence and respond accordingly, so try to show up for at least a few minutes every day. You can set your notifications to alert you by email when someone comments on your page.

Analytics: In your page's admin panel you'll see a tab with a graph showing both your reach and audience engagement levels. Click *See All* to view the full analytics for your page. Pay attention to which posts have more virality and adjust your offerings accordingly, or else use the engage tips above to find people interested in what you offer. Adjusting your page's reach to the ideal audience for you is a trial-by-error process.

Promoting from Your Page

While it is possible to promote from your page, you should do so cautiously. Spamming doesn't work and will only cause you to lose followers. Be subtle and lure rather than pursue readers.

I received a bit of free advertising money from Facebook, so I decided to try out a couple of ads. My results indicate that the same easy-does-it guidelines apply to ads, too. The campaign I ran as an inline ad with a post of my book video did far better than the promoted posts ad with a cover of my book and a promotional blurb.

My observation is that people are on Facebook to socialize and have fun, not to be pitched to. Consider using this site as a primary outpost if you work well in that kind of environment and can promote in a subtle manner.

FOURTEEN

12 Reasons for Writers to Love Facebook

Becky Johnson

True Confession: For me, Facebook was love at first post.

Apparently I am not alone. Facebook reigns as Social Media King, with more than a billion active users. Here are a dozen reasons why Facebook is this writer's Social Networking BFF.

1. Cure for Isolation: I am a relational gal and it is no secret that writing can be an isolating business. Facebook is a 24 Hour Kitchen Table "Come and Go" Conversation that never ends. I can connect to other writers who are also trapped at home on a deadline. In fact, Facebook is a virtual water cooler for thousands who work at home in their PJs but enjoy a little human connection with their coffee break.

2. Primes My Writing Pump: I read Facebook the way some read the morning paper (before newspapers all but disappeared). I like to peruse my friends' thoughts while I sip my coffee. Writing a comment here, a question there, gets my writer's juices flowing. Before long I fill in my status, which is much less daunting than writing a first sentence on an empty page. Interacting on Facebook eases me into a writing frame of mind.

3. Testing Material: Since I write humor, Facebook is a great place to test comedic material. If I get lots of good comments, I cut and past the post into a "Humor File" to use later in a blog or book.

4. Finding Topics that Hit a Nerve: Recently my daughter wrote a FB status about the pros and cons of when to share news of a pregnancy. More than 300 passionate responses from readers later, Rachel knew she'd stumbled upon a hot topic for her blog (www.thenourishedmama.com).

5. Easy Daily Journal: Everyone knows writers should journal daily. But what with all the social media we are now required to do to build our platform, who has time to journal, too? It's a comfort to me that I have recorded the highlights of my experiences in a brief (publicly read) journal over the last five years . . . on Facebook. Romance novelist Eloisa James wrote an entire memoir *(Paris in Love)* based on a year of Facebook posts! Because the posts were so well written, to my surprise, the book was hard to put down.

6. Gathering Ideas from Readers: In her bestselling book *The Happiness Project,* Gretchen Rubin sprinkles short tips and thoughts from her blog readers' comments throughout the book. This added interest and variety to her book, especially when presented in bullet-point format.

7. Finding Original Quotes, Quips, and Anecdotes from Others: I wrote a couple of Facebook posts during a vacation when my husband and I both caught the flu. An author friend, writing a book on marriage, asked if she could use my posts as anecdotal material. I was happy to share; and she was gracious to attribute the quotes to me and mention my latest books as a reference in her book. A win-win!

8. Practicing "Writing Tight": Today's internet-skimming readers don't have patience for long, meandering prose. Writing short FB posts is terrific practice in the art of writing tight. Today's writers must know how to nutshell and extract worthwhile thoughts with as few words as possible. This past week I experienced two incredibly fun hours at a birthday party with four of my grandsons. Rather than bore my friends with a blow-by-blow account of my adorable grandchildren, I posted: "I went to a birthday party at a skating rink today and did the hokey pokey with four of my grandsons. And that's what it's all about."

9. Facebook Friends Are Faithful Fans: I've discovered Facebook friends to be faithful supporters of my blogs and books, generous in helping get the word out by re-posting press releases, book sales, and good reviews.

10. Networking: You never know how a Facebook relationship can lead to opportunities for writing or marketing your book. My daughter struck up a friendship with another prolific blogger who asked Rachel to guest post for a popular teacher's blog. Rachel did so well that she was offered a paying gig to write regularly for www.weareteachers.com. We've also landed radio, podcast, and other web interviews because someone in media saw and liked our posts, blogs, or book topic on Facebook.

11. Random Polls: In our book *Nourished: A Search for Health, Happiness and a Full Night's Sleep* (Zondervan, 2015), my daughter (and co-author) wanted to address the Top 10 Everyday Stressors Women Face. So I posted the question, "What are the daily things that slow you down, trip you up, and steal your peace?" We gathered dozens of replies and categorized them into 10 areas that formed the basis for an entire book.

12. A Word for the Weary: How often have I received the perfect word of encouragement, comfort, or advice from someone on Facebook, exactly when I needed it? I've also had the privilege of regularly encouraging others via Facebook. For those who welcome it, Facebook connections can be a true ministry of words, whether or not you are professionally published.

FIFTEEN

Facebook: Friend or Enemy?

Jan Drexler

Facebook. So what *IS* it about marketing on Facebook that makes us all cringe? I know I'm not the only one who wants to forget about it and get to work writing my next book!

But after a couple of valuable appointments with marketing gurus at the ACFW conference in September, I started looking at Facebook a little differently. It is part of our lives, and it can be a valuable asset to our writing careers.

Here are some things I've learned:

Treat both your author page and your personal page the same. Both of them are seen by your readers and potential readers. Once you're a published author, you don't have a private life on the internet. If you aren't published yet, act as if you are!

Stick to your brand. I write historical romance books. Most of them are Amish, with a foray into a western being published by Love Inspired next year. On my Facebook author page, I share Amish tidbits plus a fun picture of cowboys once in a while. That's what my readers expect, and I try not to disappoint them! And yes, when I have news about one of my books, I'll post about that, too. But that kind of post is rare.

Post regularly. Some authors use a service like Hootsuite to schedule their Facebook posts, but I've found that I like to fly by the seat of my pants when posting on my author page. I try to post at least once a day, only because that drives up traffic. Regularity is a key to reaching larger numbers of my readers.

Understand that even if you aren't a public figure now, you will be. (At least that's the goal, right?) As you're sharing all about your dogs, grandchildren or passion for hanggliding, don't forget to insert a layer of protection between you and your reading public. Certain things need to be kept private. You can give your readers quite a bit of information about your life—and let them feel like they know you—without divulging every detail.

Be friendly. Whether on your personal Facebook page or your professional one, the personal distance you need to maintain shouldn't keep you from giving your readers a genuine smile of welcome when they drop by. Let your voice shine through. Be inviting. Make them want to spend time with you in your books.

Be professional. Facebook is not the place to air dirty laundry, complain about or celebrate political events, or argue theological differences. Never, ever complain about your spouse, children, in-laws, bosses, or co-workers. And never, never, never (can't say enough nevers!) complain about or divulge information about editors, agents, or anyone else in the writing business. What appears on the internet has a horribly tenacious way of sticking around.

Be a good neighbor. Don't you love when your peers share your latest status with all of their friends? Especially when you're trying to pull readers to your latest blog post or publicize the sale price on one of your books? Do the same for them.

Sometimes I think of Facebook as a necessary evil, one of the many things we need to negotiate in order to be successful in this modern life. It won't last forever, but as long as it's around, we should use it to our advantage. And meanwhile, enjoy it!

SIXTEEN

To Tweet or Not to Tweet (The Social Media Platform Question)

Janalyn Voigt

Twitter is a top social network and one of the sites a prospective agent or publisher is likely to check when evaluating a writer's online presence. This factor alone makes it worth investigating, but there's more. Once you understand how to use it properly, Twitter can drive traffic to your site and customers to your books.

What is Twitter?

Twitter is an information network with real-time immediacy. Trending stories often break first on Twitter. It's also a social networking platform where people from all over the world post short updates. Tweets take little time to compose. Your wall, made up of brief tweets, is quick to scan. On Twitter you can create lists of people and make them public or private. It's possible to join ongoing group conversations (like #AmWriting or #WriteTip). If you have a Facebook account, this should all sound familiar. Think of Twitter as "Facebook Light."

Because of the character limitations (just 140 characters per tweet), you don't need to spend a lot of time maintaining Twitter. Tweets cover, among other things, personal updates, conversations, commentaries on something in the news, interesting posts, original limericks, and even entire books painstakingly tweeted in numbered, sequential order. When it comes to composing Twitter updates, you're only limited by your imagination.

Tweets can be prescheduled via social media dashboards like Tweetdeck, Social Oomph, Buffer, and Hootsuite. I have used all of these at one time or another and now use them all for different features. There's also Twuffer, which I have not tried, but many people swear by it. Which you choose is really a matter of preference. I suggest you start out with Hootsuite, since its interface is easiest for the beginner. As a bonus, you can schedule updates for Facebook, Google+, and LinkedIn through Hootsuite as well. I use the URL shortener at Bitly.com and also via Buffer because these sites give me the ability to track analytics for the links I post.

Getting Started on Twitter?

For branding purposes and to present yourself as professional, I suggest you *use your author name as your handle.* Capitalize your first and last name for better readability. My twitter handle, for example, is @JanalynVoigt rather than @janalynvoigt.

Be sure to upload a profile image. Many people, myself included, won't follow accounts without a profile picture because this is a telltale sign of a spammer.

Don't be afraid to poke around Twitter and familiarize yourself with its many aspects. Third-party Twitter applications abound, but don't get carried away discovering them or you may burn out on Twitter before you start. It's best to start simple. Also, be careful when it comes to third-party applications. They shouldn't need your email address or Twitter password to function. After you've granted permission to an application to access your account, if you don't intend to use it again, it's always a good idea to go into your Twitter settings through the gear icon on your profile page, select apps from the menu on the left, and revoke its access to your account.

What if you just don't "get" Twitter?

I truly understand the confusion of not knowing how to relate to others on Twitter. It took me several years to truly grasp how to use this particular social platform. I might not have kept trying except that much of my website traffic came from updates about my blog posts that I made to Twitter. I only wish I'd discovered sooner that the character of my interactions, rather than the nature of Twitter, was the problem. Accusing Twitter for my failure to connect through it was akin to blaming a forest fire on a careless camper's match. For those who persevere, Twitter can prove quite a powerhouse.

I didn't consciously decide to use Twitter as an outlet to promote my writing without investing anything of myself in my followers. In fact, I tried periodically to get people to "talk to me," but I wasn't successful. I first had to figure out some basics, and I'm happy to share them with you.

To get people to talk to me on Twitter, I:

- **joined hashtag conversations.** These sound complicated but aren't. Twitter communications can seem disjointed, so hashtag conversations arose out of the need to organize tweets into cohesive group conversations. To see how this works, type #AmWriting (a popular hashtag conversation for writers) into the search box on Twitter. To add to the conversation, simply include #AmWriting in your own tweet. Taking part in hashtag conversations helps you find people who are active on Twitter.

- **paid attention to who followed me and followed them back if possible.** Several good applications for managing your Twitter followers exist, including Friend or Follow and Manage Flitter. These sites let you easily do things like follow people back and un-follow those who aren't following you (if you wish). I don't always follow those who follow me. Some are on Twitter to promote businesses that don't interest me or are engaged in activities I don't want to endorse. If we'll have nothing in common to talk about, I don't follow back. Engagement is far more important than large numbers of followers.

- **tweeted blog posts written by others and included their Twitter handle** (user name preceded by the @ sign—mine is @JanalynVoigt). This prevents your tweet with a link from being considered spam and no-tifies persons with the handles you include that you mentioned them. Often those we do favors for will look for ways to return those favors, but I don't do it for that reason or look for a return. I tweet relevant links of in-terest to my followers to keep them engaged with me.

- **retweeted (tweeted again) posts of interest to my niche.** This helps me interact with others, feed inter-esting updates to my followers, and gain new followers.

- **consciously following other people I knew.** I pro-actively searched out my friends who are on Twitter. We're already invested in and support one another, and I know these people will talk to me.

- **mentioned people and thanked them when they mentioned me.** Twitter has #FollowFriday, also known as #FF, that's gotten a bit out of hand, but if used right is a viable way to recommend people you want to help and gain followers as others help you. Basically, every Friday people on Twitter recommend some of their favorite followers by listing their Twitter handles with the #FF or #FollowFriday hashtags included in the tweet. Using the @ symbol before a person's handle causes the name to become a link that takes your followers who click it to that person's profile. You don't have to use the #FollowFriday hashtag to follow people, though. You can mention them whenever you want.

- **when time allowed, I spent a few minutes looking over websites and commenting about them to people who interested me.** This communicates that I'm interested in the person, and sometimes I find material to tweet to my followers.

- **began scheduling regular updates.** Don't get carried away posting updates, but most people post too seldom rather than too often. I try to update my Twitter profile using prescheduled tweets once an hour. We've discussed scheduling updates, but you can also automatically feed blog posts to Twitter through Twitter Feed and Mail Chimp.

There's truth to the idea that those who aren't using Twitter can't understand it and those on Twitter can't explain it. To decide whether Twitter is or isn't for you, why not give it a try?

SEVENTEEN

How a Blue Bird Can Save You Time

Jan Dunlap

I love Twitter.

Yes, it's true—a few years ago, I said I would never get on Twitter.

Just like I said "no Facebook," the year before that.

The truth is that as an author, if you're not on the social networks, you're missing the boat, and while I'm still learning the best ways to use social media, I've found a surprising, but HUGE, benefit to spending time every day on Twitter: it's my go-to source for content.

Content—the endless supply of information you need to share—is one of the things you have to manage on social media, and for me, it was one of the most intimidating. I barely eke out enough time to work on manuscripts between book marketing, my part-time teaching job, mothering, housekeeping, and walking the dog, let alone to come up with bright new pieces of information to post on my social networks every day. Effective social media marketing requires new content to keep your followers interested in what you do as an author; if your audience doesn't hear from you in a while, they'll move on to someone or something new, which defeats your whole social media strategy.

On top of fresh material, I also have to find or create the right spin on the content I collect to make it appropriate for my social networks. My readers expect humor, which isn't nearly as simple or easy as it may sound; all authors—no matter what they write about—have to somehow personalize the content they curate to reflect their own signature brand.

Enter Twitter—tiny snippets of titles on anything and everything. It's like an overflowing cornucopia of trivia, which is exactly what I like about it—I can skim through my Twitter feed and if some title catches my eye and strikes me as funny, or inspires a witty response in me, I can open the link and immediately bookmark it into a folder on my laptop. (Keeping a bookmarking folder dedicated to raw social media content has been one of my better ideas.) Then, when I'm making the rounds on my social networks and need new content, I can open that folder and retrieve the snippet for instant material. I've discovered that in just a few minutes a day, I can find enough tweets on Twitter to provide me with ideas and quick posts for a week, which frees up more time to write.

The danger of wasting time on Twitter was originally one of the reasons I didn't want to use it, because like all social media, it pulls you into engagement that is hard to escape. (How many times have you told yourself, "I'm only reading one more post," and then, an hour later, you're still on Facebook?) By mindfully turning my Twitter time into content development time, I've made it a more productive and focused task that actually reduces the amount of time I need to spend on creating posts for my other networks. And that makes me *tweet* with happiness! (And you can join me @BirderMurder!)

EIGHTEEN

What is "Take Away" Value?

Dineen Miller

In order to successfully sell our books, we need to have "take away" value. Sometimes that's pretty obvious, but other times it's as subtle as how you're presenting your product or services. I find at times it's a fine line that we can easily cross into the "me" zone.

I have a feeling, though, that you've seen and know what that looks like. How about Twitter? I get a fair amount of requests but have little time to follow people who are just throwing stuff out there for the sake of being visible. Plus, I want to follow people that I can relate to and connect with. I'm most likely not going to follow a furniture company located in a different state.

Except, this time I did. Why?

Take a look at the Twitter page for Mealey's Furniture, (@FollowMealeys) located in Warminster, PA. They do a lot of things right.

1. They don't over-tweet. Mealey's tweets about two to three times a day. When I see a Twitter page loaded with hourly tweets of stuff just thrown out there, I'm not going to pay attention. The delete button is my friend.

2. Their tweets are helpful. They have take away value. Not only do they have it, they personalize it. They're not just putting tweets out there about a sale, they're

giving you decorating ideas and hints for better living. They also support causes. Basically, they don't want to just sell you a piece of furniture. They want to add quality to your life. Again, motivation is key.

3. They're not just about the product. Mealey's presence is clearly not about them. They are about the customer and serving those needs. They're focused on their audience and serving them, not on themselves.

This is brilliant marketing. Would I buy furniture from Mealey's? If they had a store in San Jose, CA, you bet they'd be the first place I'd think of next time I needed something.

The key here is they make a lasting and positive impression. You walk away from this page with the understanding that to them, it's not just about the sale. They want to do more for their customers. They want to connect with them.

Today's market takes more than just what we have to offer, which in nonfiction is a lot. We have a clear message, an idea, or something to share. But there's already so much out there. We have to be clear about the "why." Think about why we write what we write and how we can translate that into connecting with our readers, which in turn translates into word-of-mouth marketing—the best kind. Just as I'm talking about Mealey's furniture because they offered me take away value, we want our readers to talk about our books, our message, and what we stand for.

But even that comes back to our motivation. Are we doing it to just sell books? Or are we, like Mealey's, genuinely trying to give quality to our readers? That's our origination point in writing these books to help others. Let's not leave that motivation in the pages of our books. Let's figure out ways we can we bring that over into our marketing too.

NINETEEN

Should You Be On Pinterest?

Janalyn Voigt

The trouble with being a writer is that you have to write. That would seem desirable, but the writing I'm talking about goes beyond pounding out the next scene in my novel. Since becoming a published novelist, I've submitted—at the request of agents, editors, bloggers, and marketing personnel—guest posts, interview responses, pitch sentences, two-sentence blurbs, query letters, proposals, sample chapters, material to use for promotion, back-cover copy, tag lines, book club questions, and of course myriad versions of my biography. Add to this the need to devise creative updates for social networks, and you begin to see why a writer might groan.

Enter Pinterest, a social media platform that allows members to network with pictures more than words. I love writing and (go figure) even have a fondness for words, but I find Pinterest a breath of fresh air. As a virtual bulletin board where users pin images, Pinterest frees me to express my creativity without having to hurt my brain with so much thinking. Since women primarily frequent Pinterest, spending more time on it than on other networks, it provides another benefit. Book buyers are predominantly female. (This varies by genre.)

With 4 million active daily visitors and as the fastest-growing social media site (now second only to Facebook), Pinterest is a site many writers should include in their social media platforms. Since I began to take Pinterest seriously, it's moved to the number one referrer of traffic to my websites.

I won't go into detail on how to sign up, since Pinterest makes it easy. If you want advice, visit the Pinterest Help Center and enter "how to sign up" in the search box. I suggest you set up or convert to a Pinterest business account. This will allow you access to account analytics once you verify your website for Pinterest.

Be sure and include your author picture in your profile. Also set up a branded bio. This is a little challenging since you should make it brief so it will be read. Every word needs to pull its weight. To see an example, visit the Pinterest page for Janalyn Voigt. While you're there, take a look at my boards to help inspire your own.

Pinterest Goodies

After you've created your account, filled in your profile information, and verified your website, you should visit Pinterest's Goodies page. There you'll find instructions on how to:

- install the Pin It button (for Google Chrome) to your bookmark bar.
- drag the Pinterest Bookmarklet to your toolbar (click the red link under the Pin It button copy in the sentence that says: "Looking for the Pinterest Bookmarklet?").
- add a Pin It button to your site.
- make a widget for your site.

Creating Your Boards:

On your profile page, you'll be able to create boards. Here are some suggestions:

- Name a board for your blog or website.
- Create a board with the title of your book(s).

- Name a board for the genre(s) you write.
- Think up boards that will reinforce your brand.
- Design boards to attract your target audience.

Pin Three Ways

- Click the Pinterest bookmarklet while at a website that grants permission to pin its images and select the image you want to pin.
- Under your image in the Pinterest toolbar you'll find a dropdown menu. Click "Add Pin" to upload an image from your computer or enter the URL of a picture you have permission to pin.
- Use the Pin It button on a website.

What to Pin

- Pin your own original images with a link back to your site.
- Pin images from sites that state they allow pinning to Pinterest.
- Pin public-domain images.
- Create and pin your own collages using sites like Picmonkey.com and your own images.

What to Do on Pinterest

- **Follow other people.** You can choose to follow all boards or an individual board. As with all effective social networking, be sincere. When you make the effort to follow people, some will follow you back.
- **Repin from boards of people you trust.** Always verify that the link goes where the image indicates it will and that the original site gave permission to pin.
- **Like pins others post.** This brings you to their attention.

- **Comment on pins.** To comment, click on a pin and the comment box will be in the enlarged image that displays.

Pinterest and Copyright

First, I am not a lawyer and don't mean the following in any way as legal advice, but here is how I handle myself on Pinterest. I'm careful when pinning images that I don't own to make sure the website gives explicit permission to pin to Pinterest in its copyright policy. I don't take the existence of a Pin It button as permission. I'm aware that even if I own a photo, some things like private works of art or images of people who have not signed a release for me to post their photos, for example, are off limits. I prefer to take my own photographs and create my own infographics. When in doubt, I don't pin.

Pinterest is a relatively painless way to network that is actually a lot of fun It can help you keep track of research while simultaneously drawing readers to your books.

TWENTY

LinkedIn for Writers

Janalyn Voigt

When deciding where to focus online, most writers veer toward Facebook, Twitter, and Pinterest. Developing a presence at those sites can be a great idea. However, with almost 450 million users worldwide, LinkedIn carries a clout all its own. Chances are you think of LinkedIn as a network for job seekers, and while it does function in that capacity, it offers other benefits to writers.

Reach Readers

Although LinkedIn's focus is business-to-business, don't discount it as an avenue to reach readers. I personally experienced a spike in book sales after putting the word out on LinkedIn about *DawnSinger* (Tales of Faeraven 1). The link I posted had a lot of shares, which means my network kicked in to help. As members of my network shared my update to their networks, they increased its impact exponentially, creating additional exposure for my book. This is social networking at its best. Just remember that giving more than you receive will help you tap its power. (It's also a great way to live.)

Extend Your Network

LinkedIn allows you to introduce yourself to those in the networks of your network. This can be a powerful tool for growing your sphere of influence. Be careful about approaching agents and editors this way, though. It's best to send them a contact request after an in-person meeting.

Give and Receive Endorsements

LinkedIn lets you easily endorse people you respect for their professional skills. This also means that others can do the same for you. While you can request that others endorse you, use this tool wisely. If people don't know you or your work, don't send them an endorsement request.

Discover Who Views Your Profile

It's fun to click a sidebar link and discover who has recently visited your profile. While those who upgrade to a professional account receive more information, even those who use a free plan can see a few names. As an example, recent visitors to the LinkedIn profile for Janalyn Voigt included a librarian, another author and speaker, a digital publisher, a barbershop manager, and a Los Angeles-based writer and editor. In the past I've also caught a film producer and agent checking out my profile. These people can represent contacts you may want to follow up with.

Link Your Blog

LinkedIn's blog link tool enables you to feed your blog to your LinkedIn profile. This helps you brand while giving your blog additional reach.

Automatically Update from Twitter

Feed your Twitter updates to LinkedIn. Go to settings to enable this feature.

Conduct Polls

Use the LinkedIn polls application to gain insights that can help you determine what to write, how to promote, and where to find your target audience. You can integrate your LinkedIn polls to Facebook or Twitter and also embed them in your website.

Improve Your Website's SEO

Be sure to include a link to your website and/or blog in your profile. Garnering links back to your blog from high-authority sites helps raise its visibility in search engines. A good search-engine ranking means that when people search the internet for keywords within your topic, your site shows as close as possible to the first page of their results. This is known as search engine optimization, or SEO.

Focus on Business

One of my author friends centers his online social networking at LinkedIn more than at other sites. When I asked him why he prefers LinkedIn, he answered that it's all business. Since he's had to break himself of an online gaming habit, this makes sense for him. LinkedIn's business focus extends even further than not featuring games, and that's good news for writers in a lot of ways. On LinkedIn you don't "friend" or "follow" people, you add them into your network. Having an established network means that you can connect on a strictly-business level with (to name a few) publishing professionals (such as agents and editors), experts in fields you need to research, technical experts who design websites or make book trailers, and other authors willing to cross-promote.

Join Relevant Groups

LinkedIn is another place to connect with others on topics of interest to your author brand. You can also participate in groups of writers to talk shop. As an example, I've used LinkedIn groups to compare notes with other writers in an effort to discover where to focus promotional efforts. A simple search on LinkedIn will turn up groups to consider joining.

Follow Publishing Houses and Agencies

Use the 'follow companies' LinkedIn feature to keep tabs on publishing houses and agencies. As a bonus, you can see how you are connected to these companies, which can give you contact leads.

How to Proceed with LinkedIn

Start by creating a free account, and then fill in your profile completely, using targeted keywords (see the section above on improving website SEO). Once you've done this, send invitations to connect with all your contacts and concentrate on growing your network in the ways mentioned throughout this post. I'm sure you'll agree that LinkedIn is a powerhouse for writers.

TWENTY-ONE

I'm Hooked on LinkedIn

Jan Dunlap

After three years of experimenting with social media networking, I'm finally closing in on what works best for my marketing needs at this time.

But before I share with you what I've discovered, I need to make some qualifications of phrases in that first sentence.

1. **'Experimenting'** – I've had no formal training in using Facebook, Twitter, LinkedIn, Google+, or Pinterest. Instead, I've read countless books and blog posts about using them, taken online webinars and asked others what they do. I've tried some ideas (mostly the ones I understood how to do) and rejected others (the ones I had no idea how to do). My experimenting has truly been all over the net, kind of like sampling all the flavors in an ice cream shop—a small bite at a time.

2. **'Works best'** – I define this as 'what I can successfully manage, given limited time and ability because I am not a social media guru, nor do I aspire to become one.'

3. **'Marketing needs'** – For me, this is publicity and audience building. I don't sell books myself; I focus on branding myself to create the desire in my audience to go to vendors. *Ultimately, I want my audience to become my sales team to sell my books to others, since there are a lot more of them than there is of me!*

4. **'At this time'** – Marketing needs change over time, as do the ways different media platforms function. I dread every announcement that a social site has made 'changes,' because it means I have to learn/relearn how to use it.

All that said, I have found MY most successful audience builder to be LinkedIn. That's because I focus there on connecting with others who work professionally in the fields in which I write: dogs, birds, health and wellness.

Yes, you read that right—my *Birder Murder Mysteries* and girl-meets-dog memoir appeal to three audiences, yet they overlap because my overarching brand is about getting outside to get healthier and happier. My contacts are working professionals at state parks, dog- or bird-related businesses, wellness advocates, animal rescue groups, and ecotourism, to name a few. My strategy is to strengthen my social relationships with those contacts by engaging in conversations with them individually and collectively, which is what LinkedIn shines at. I see my contacts as distribution points—when I engage them meaningfully, they share my brand/message/content with their own networks. **And LinkedIn makes it easy for me to find people who already care about my topic(s) with their group listings and recommendations**.

My marketing strategy will continue to evolve, as healthy marketing strategies do, and I know that my experimentation with other networks is far from over. For now, though, LinkedIn is the backbone of my social networking strategy since it yields me the most new contacts, opportunities to market, and book sales numbers of all the platforms.

TWENTY-TWO

Google Plus for Writers

Janalyn Voigt

Google+ offers unique benefits for writers wise enough to take advantage of them. Why do we need another social site when there's already Facebook, LinkedIn, and Twitter? While these social sites are great networking tools, they don't have all the capabilities of Google+.

Another consideration is cost. Only a fraction of those who sign up to receive your Facebook updates are allowed to see them. Facebook will extend your reach, but at a cost. Google+ lets you contact those in your circles free of charge.

Interest communities can help you find readers.

One of the things that Google+ does best is to connect people with similar interests. You can search for groups, start a group, and manage your groups.

Increase your discoverability.

Updates you make to Google+ rank well in Google's search engine. This puts your updates higher in results for relevant search terms. This can make you as an author more visible to readers.

Create videos, host author chats and network through Google hangouts.

Up to ten people can connect through hangouts. Through its **Hangouts on Air** capabilities, Google+ gives authors a free and easy way to broadcast live. Better yet, it then can automatically update your Google+ home page and YouTube account. You can also embed your videos on your website or blog. Best of all, you don't need technical skills to get in on this.

Lets you sign up for Google Authorship.

You may have wondered how images of some authors appear in search engine results, like the one below.

7. About **Janalyn Voigt** | Live Write Breathe
livewritebreathe.com/about-janalyn/ ▾
by Janalyn Voigt - in 1,049 Google+ circles
Janalyn Irene Voigt **Janalyn Voigt** credits her father with instilling a love of literature in her at an early age by reading chapters from The Wizard of Oz, Robinson ...

Your image, tagline, and most recent update will appear in the sidebar for searches of your name. This can be an important advantage if you have a popular name. The fact that Google shows my follower count helps my credibility.

To learn more about the advantages of Google Authorship, read "10 Reasons Writers Should Claim Their Google Authorship Markup" by Demian Farnworth on the blog Copyblogger (www.copyblogger.com).

Don't make the mistake of overlooking Google Plus in building your social media platform.

TWENTY-THREE

Goodreads for Writers

Janalyn Voigt

D o you daydream about a massive virtual library where lovers of books rub shoulders and authors receive free privileges and promotional opportunities? Well, dream no more. Such a site exists. Surprisingly, many writers ignore Goodreads.

A basic membership affords even unpublished writers the opportunity to include a photo and profile information, make friends with readers and other writers, share book recommendations and reviews, create their own virtual bookshelves. and join groups and forums (including groups of readers who love books in their genres).

Published authors can add the following privileges:

Author Page

It's likely you will find your book by title in the site's database. If you don't find it, it's not too difficult to add it using the "Find Books" tab. Once you locate your book, you will find a link that asks whether you're the writer of the book. Click that and follow instructions to set up your Author Page.

Bio

On your author page, you can include a biography and list your books, link to your website and blog, indicate your genre(s), and upload a picture. Take pains with this information, since visitors to your page will notice it before they scroll down to read anything else.

Blog

You can blog right in Goodreads or automatically feed updates from external blogs to your page and into the news feeds of your friends and fans. The whole post won't appear, but just the first few paragraphs with a link to your blog site. This is one way to lead readers back to your website and expose them to purchase information for your book.

Events

You can list events like your release date, blog tour stops, or book signing schedule to keep your friends and fans informed.

Videos

Set book videos, author interviews, book readings, or other promotional videos from YouTube or another online video service to display right on your Author Page.

Writing Samples

If you have an author page, you can include samples of your writing and reviews of your books for others to read.

Quotes

You can share favorite quotes from books you love, including your own! Give readers a taste of your writing and they may just purchase your book and keep on reading.

Fans

Your Author Page includes a place where readers can sign up to be your fans. You will then appear in the "Favorite Authors" section of their profiles and they will receive updates from your Author Page.

Status Updates

Goodreads has a status update box that allows you 240 characters to comment on topics of your choice. Your update will show up in the newsfeeds of your friends and fans. Starting a discussion about an author who writes books similar to yours is a great way to engage with readers who might also enjoy your books. The update box is a little difficult to find. In the top menu bar, click "home," and then look in the right sidebar for the text link entitled "general update" under the "what are you reading" header. Click the link and an update box should appear.

Groups and Forums

Join reader groups and enter into their discussions to connect with readers within your genre. Remember, though, not to push your books. Engage readers by joining in the discussions at hand and they may click on your name link to go to your Author Page and find out all about you and your books.

Giveaways

If it's still within six months after your book's release date, you can set up a giveaway of your book through the "First Reads" program. This gives you the opportunity to put a brief synopsis in front of those who participate.

Special Strategies

The way Goodreads is set up yields intelligence data for authors. For instance, you can find a book similar to your own, click on its title, and learn which of your friends and fans have read it. You can search for a similar book and find active discussions about it in reader groups.

TWENTY-FOUR

Becoming Social Media Savvy

Christina M. H. Powell

If you want to become a published author in today's world, you need to embrace social media. Some aspiring authors may be very comfortable with social media and already have a large and successful online platform. However, many people preparing to write their first book may have a platform established in another way, such as through teaching, speaking, or published articles, and the world of social media may be foreign to them.

Here are a few tips for new authors looking to expand their social media presence:

1. Consider your overall social media needs. Most new authors have careers in addition to their writing. While in many cases your writing may be an outgrowth of your career, sometimes the social media needs of your career may conflict with the social media needs of your writing platform. Consider how you can achieve a workable compromise between the two. Perhaps you work in a career where a limited social media presence based solely on professional accomplishments would be ideal. However, your writing platform may thrive if you develop a more personable social media presence that lets your readers share in some details from your daily life. Maybe you can connect with work colleagues on a platform such as LinkedIn, while using

Twitter, Facebook, Goodreads, Instagram, and Google+ to connect with readers. Find what works for you, and modify your social media presence as necessary.

2. Create layers of social media connection. Before deciding to become an author, you may have used social media as a means of connecting with friends and family. Now you find that your literary agent and your publisher want you to connect with readers through social media. Connecting with readers requires a public social media presence. However, privacy controls on social media sites such as Facebook allow you to keep your posts to friends and family private while creating new posts for the general public. Using privacy controls, you can create layers of social media connection, sharing photos of your children with close friends and family members while sharing photos of book-signing events with the whole world. You might want to create a Facebook page with all posts public to connect with readers, while using your Facebook profile to connect with friends. However, consider leaving some posts from your Facebook profile public for readers who find you through a Facebook search.

3. Adapt your social media strategy to stay current. All social media sites are constantly changing, especially platforms such as Facebook, where signs around the company's campus remind employees that "this journey is only 1 percent finished." After a major update on one of your social media sites, check privacy settings, and revisit your approach to social media. Is there a great new feature that you should start using? Should you publish more videos, or schedule posts for a different time of day? As an author, your journey in the world of social media is only 1 percent finished. Learn from your past experiences on social media and the wisdom of other writers, and create fresh content using new tools and the latest technology.

TWENTY-FIVE

How to Maximize Your Social Media Time

Jordyn Redwood

Early in my wanting-to-pursue-publication journey, I heard a woman give a talk about maximizing your time. She said, "Nothing you do should go to waste. If I see a movie, I'll figure out a way to use it in my writing. I'll write something about it."

Honestly, at first, I did kind of give a big eye roll. Really? Nothing could be sacred, private, and free? Couldn't my mind ever just have a void where I didn't have to think about marketing?

Now, I might have changed my opinion on that somewhat.

Marketing is hard work. Author Richard Mabry once said to me, "It's a marathon, not a sprint." And this is the truth. When your book releases, there is usually a flurry of activity to launch your baby. But, there comes a time when you need to begin to focus on the next book while still keeping your other marketing activities going. This may be less about your book and more about growing your platform and social media presence.

Consider all your activities: can they aid in growing your social media? Can they give you a blog topic? Can something you do for fun give you a possible return on your time investment?

I recently read the book *Fear Nothing,* by Lisa Gardner. I wanted to read this book. Lisa is a favorite author of mine so I put most other books aside to enjoy her new releases.

On the marketing side, this is how I used my leisure time to help my social media.

1. I wrote a Goodreads review on the novel. This is good for authors. It gives people an example of your writing style and can help readers find you. After all, you likely write what you like to read.

2. I pinned it to Pinterest. Some readers/followers are more visual and I do find people repinning books from my boards.

3. I blogged about it– in *two* different places. My main blog is Redwood's Medical Edge, and it deals with medical accuracy in fiction. *Fear Nothing* had a character with congenital insensitivity to pain so not only did I blog about this particular medical disorder but I also did a post that was a review of the novel and some of its medical aspects. And now, I'm here blogging about how to use one activity to foster multiple marketing efforts. So, I guess that's *three* blog posts.

Your activities should become the ultimate wardrobe, where all pieces can be mixed with one another. Ultimately, a book I read for fun ended up being used to build my platform (a medical nerd who writes suspense novels) and, hopefully, keep up interest in my social media.

TWENTY-SIX

Keywording 101 for SEO Prowess

Erin MacPherson

Three words: **Search Engine Optimization**. They kind of make you want to grab a bag and start hyperventilating, don't they?

In the world of viral marketing, social media and Google Adwords, SEO has become another one of the things that you've probably had to put on your to-do list. And, if you're anything like most of the writers I talk to, you probably have no idea where to start.

I was lucky. Before I got my book deal, I'd spent five years working as a staff writer for a major media company. And, since we wrote for the web, I spent hours each week honing my SEO skills. We actually had a team of SEO gurus on staff that hosted weekly SEO boot camps for us—analyzing every article we wrote for SEO viability and nitpicking every teeny tiny keyword on our site. So, while viral marketing and blogging were new to me, I had the SEO thing down pat.

And, I have to say, it's worked for me. While I spend very little time doing viral marketing on my blog—I'm just not a good twitterer—I get fairly decent traffic—and most of it comes from Google referrals. I chalk that up to having a strong SEO strategy—and knowing where to focus my SEO time.

Obviously, SEO is a tough nut to crack—and there's no way I can give you even a tenth of the information you need in one post. Before you create a viable SEO strategy, you'll need to decide if SEO is even worth your time (in some cases, it's not), how you'll use SEO keywords (there are many, many ways that go way beyond simply keywording a post) and how to create relevancy with your keywords on your site (now *that's* complicated).

But, in order to put the horse before the cart, the first thing you need to do is come up with a list of keywords that you want to use on your blog or website. This list can (and will) become your SEO cheat sheet—you'll have something to focus on, something to consult whenever you're writing a post, a start to a strategy. Here are my tips:

1. **Limit your keywords**. I've had clients who presented me with a list of 100 keywords and then asked me to help them come up with more. And, while they have the right idea in that they are focusing on specific words instead of just throwing out a random slew of words as they write a post—they are biting off too big of a chunk. While the Google and Bing algorithms are super complicated, one important aspect is that they search for relevancy—which means in a nutshell they'll be crawling your site to see how much information on your site is relevant to a specific keyword or idea. So, unless you're posting dozens of articles every week that are very specifically focusing on all 100 of your keywords, you're probably not you're not creating a sense of relevancy with many of them. So, choose a short list (my recommendation: between 5 and 15) of keywords that you can focus on with every post, every page, and every

idea. By simplifying, you'll actually create a bigger reach.

2. **Do your research.** Don't just guess on which keywords people are searching! I use Google Adwords all the time to help my clients (and myself!) find appropriate words to focus on. They're pretty straightforward tools so you can probably figure out how to use them to your advantage in less than ten minutes.

3. **Know your competition.** Remember how I told you that I used to work for a major media website with huge traffic numbers? And remember how I said we had an entire SEO team on staff? Let me give it to you straight: Unless your last name is Grisham or you have a staff of 40 writers and editors helping you with your blog, you CANNOT compete with major sites like that. It's a waste of your time to try. Case in point: Me! My book, *The Christian Mama's Guide to Having a Baby*, is a pregnancy guide—but I have never spent even a minute focusing on the keywords "pregnancy," "pregnancy book" or "pregnancy guide." Why? Have you ever heard of *What to Expect When You're Expecting?* Or *Baby Center?* I could spend hours a week creating relevancy on my site around the word "pregnancy" and only move from page 120,000 to page 50,000 on Google. And, while moving up 70,000 pages is pretty good, I'm pretty sure no one has ever looked past the first two pages of Google results, so it's absolutely a waste of my time to focus on "pregnancy." Instead, choose words that get a decent number of searches every month (target: between 1,000-10,000 global monthly searches) and low

competition (less than 20 percent on Adwords) and focus on those.

4. **If you don't talk about it on your site, don't use it as a keyword.** I see this mistake all the time . . . my clients throw out a search keyword based on a theme or idea in their books, but when I pull up their website, I see nothing about that particular idea on their website. It's not only poor user experience—if someone Googles "Amish recipes" and then comes to your site and finds nothing about Amish recipes, they're probably not going to stick around—but it also does nothing to create a sense of relevancy around that keyword, which will hurt your SEO. This does not, however, mean you need to blog only about the topics in your novels. For example, author Jody Hedlund has a wonderful blog full of tips and ideas for authors (find it at www.jodyhedlund.com)—however, her latest novel, *The Doctor's Lady*, is about the first woman to pioneer the Oregon Trail. On her website, Jody has done a great job of creating relevancy surrounding the theme of her book by creating a cool "reader fun" page that's full of facts, quizzes and more surrounding the historical times in her books. Similarly, author Rosslyn Elliot, a historical romance author who wrote *Fairer Than Morning*, maintains a "History" page on her site that adds relevancy surrounding the historical concepts in her novels.

5. **Cater to groupies.** As fun as it would be to be loved by everyone, it's just not going to happen. As a pregnancy author, I can't appease the natural birthers AND the epidural fanatics. And you can't appease everyone

either. So, think about your core audience—the people who ABSOLUTELY love everything you do—and work to appease them both with your site content and your keywords. For example, my friend Cathy West wrote an amazing historical romance called *Yesterday's Tomorrow* that's set in Vietnam during the war. And, while her book is great for all sorts of populations, you can bet that Vietnam vets and their families find it especially compelling. My recommendation for Cathy? To cater to that population, both by creating contests and posts that appeal to Vietnam vets, but also by focusing her keyword reach on words that appeal to that audience.

TWENTY-SEVEN

Keywording 201 for SEO Prowess: Three Simple To-Dos to Improve SEO

Erin MacPherson

In the previous post, I gave you the 411 on how to choose thematic keywords for your site. And, now that y'all have researched your keywords on Google Adwords, honed your theme, and come up with a strong list of 10-15 keywords (you did that, right?), you're probably wondering what to do with said list.

Using keywords correctly is complicated. Really complicated. And to be honest, figuring out the algorithm takes rocket-scientist brainpower and the ability to focus on complicated things like numbers and graphs for long stretches of time (12 minutes at least). And, since I'm guessing that doesn't sound like something you want to do when you could be doing fun things like writing, I'm going to make it really, really easy for you. So easy, in fact, that even a busy novelist with less than four minutes of free time between soccer drop-off and throwing dinner in the crockpot can get it done.

Homework caveat: Before you can complete this to-do list, you'll need to come up with a list of 10-15 thematic keywords for your blog. Refer to the previous chapter for instructions.

Three Simple To-Dos That Will Improve Your SEO

1. **Use at least ONE of your keywords in the TITLE of a blog post at least one time per week.** *(Why? Title or H1 tags—especially title tags on Wordpress, which is built for SEO—have a strong SEO value. That means that when you use a word in the title, the Google crawlers will automatically assume the article has something to do thematically with that word.)*

2. **Make a hyperlink to a different blog article on your site in each blog post you write.** BONUS: If possible, make the word that's hyperlinked be one of your keywords. For example: if your keyword is "women of faith", try to link the words "women of faith" to a separate article on your site that's about women of faith. *(Why? Just like title tags, Google crawlers assume that when your article links to another article, it has strong relevancy to that theme.)*

3. **Try to use at least one of your keywords in every article you write.** *(Why? It's the thematic relevancy thing again—the more you organically use your words, the more Google is going to assume you know what you're talking about when it comes to those themes.)*

That's it! Easy, peasy, right?

TWENTY-EIGHT

Spruce Up Your Spring Blogging Wardrobe

Michelle Griep

Tired of the same old blogging drudgery? Ready to don something light and new? Want to increase the traffic on your site? Here are a few different outfits for you to try on your blog.

VLOGGING

Everyone's got a blog, but how do you get yours to stand out? Try vlogging. A vlog is simply a video log. Instead of writing the same old, same old blog entry, you simply speak it into a camera.

Before you freak out, read my lips: this doesn't have to be fancy. In fact, I wouldn't know how to edit if you paid me. I use Photo Booth and do a vlog entry all in one shot. If you want to get fancier, though, you can use things like Microsoft Movie Maker or Apple iMovie to add all kinds of fun effects to your video.

Why should you vlog?

It's a great way to spice up your usual blog posts. It adds variety. Personally, I choose to post humorous vlogs, but you could make them "how to's" or even use them for interviews.

Vlogging is a great way to show your readers the human side of you. Your facial expressions, your inflections and intonations, are seen instead of imagined.

The other benefit I've noticed is that vlogging bumps up hits. If you're looking for a way to increase traffic, give this technique a whirl.

It's not as scary as it seems.

I'm not going to lie. The first time your knees will probably knock a fair amount, but after that, no more noodle legs. If it creeps you out to see your mug up on the screen, then here's a little tip . . . just post it. Don't watch it.

Even if you decide not to continue with vlogging on a regular basis, it's a great way to perk up your blog once and awhile.

TUMBLR

No, that's not a typo. Tumblr is a trendy way of shortening the words tumble and log. What gets tumbled? Thoughts, mostly. Think of it as a stream of consciousness, where nothing is lengthy, and randomness rules the day. On Tumblr, you'll see posts that are as simple as a link, a photo, a quote, sometimes even just a phrase.

Why use Tumblr?

This site facilitates quick and easy posting of single items. If the thought of writing blog entry after blog entry is overwhelming, this might be just the site for you. It's not a replacement for Blogger or WordPress, but an alternative for less in-depth, editorial pieces.

Plus, it's super easy to use. Setting up your own page takes about two minutes. Literally. Plus you can post from a computer, a smart phone, or yes . . . drum roll please . . . even from a text.

How to use Tumblr.

1. Sign up. Go directly to Tumblr.com and follow the directions.

2. Learn the dashboard. Your account will have a private dashboard that only you will see. This is also where you'll find the different kinds of posts that are available for you to utilize.

3. Customize your page. Make it your own. You can upload background images or use some of the free templates.

4. Start posting. The best way to figure out Tumblr is simply by putting your hands on the steering wheel and hitting the gas pedal. It's a creative place, so go ahead and run free. Try out new things you've maybe never done before, like a vlog, or post a stanza of poetry, or maybe a photo you shot recently.

5. Follow other users, kind of like Twitter. It will get your name out there in Tumblville, and eventually you'll be pulling in followers of your own.

Even if you're not quite ready to take the Tumblr plunge by setting up your own page, go ahead and check it out. It's a fun place to hang around.

TWENTY-NINE

Crowdfunding: Is It a Writer's New Marketing Tool?

Ken Gire

With the technological, social, and demographic upheavals that have happened within the publishing landscape over the last decade, many writers have found themselves having to get more involved with things that most writers hate—sales and marketing.

Myself included.

My last book sold under 500 copies, and that experience was so discouraging I felt like giving up writing entirely.

Faced with fewer and fewer bookstores to sell our books, and smaller and smaller advances to fund the writing, what's a writer to do?

There's not a lot of options, honestly, but here are a few.

Marry rich.

Consider "Breaking Bad."

Crowdfunding.

Crowdfunding is growing in popularity, and, though it has had its share of failures, it has had its share of successes, too. Numerous sites have sprung up. Kickstarter and Indiegogo are the two most popular. And there are faith-based crowdfunding platforms you can google. They are newer, less successful, and generally the funding is lower.

I first became intrigued when I found out about the almost unheard-of success in publishing with one of Seth Godin's books.

I had been following Seth's TED talks for some time, so his campaign really intrigued me. When I looked at the numbers, I had to do a double-take. Who needs that kind of money to write a book? I wondered. Then I realized what he was doing. He wasn't trying to get an advance; he was trying to generate pre-sales. And he did that through the platform of crowdfunding.

Seth is an internationally-known marketing guru, and so he probably shouldn't be used as a poster child for crowdfunding, but I used him anyway to show the possibilities.

Well, the long and short of it is . . . I decided to try it.

Though I am not the least bit tech-savvy, I managed to do it all myself, with the exception of the video. I found someone on Elance who did that for me fairly cheaply.

I also thought it would be helpful for those involved in the campaign if I gave regular updates on the progress I was making on writing my book. I remembered reading Steinbeck's, *Working Days*, a journal he kept while writing *Grapes of Wrath*, and I remember how much I enjoyed it. So I decided to write a blog (Centurion) aimed at aspiring writers so they could see what the process of writing a novel was like.

The daily posts have been really fun for me, a nice break from my writing, and also a creative outlet to try to find things on the internet that would help illustrate my blogs.

I think this could be a good option for many of us. For those of us who don't have a publisher. For those whose advance wasn't enough to finish their book. For those needing expense money to travel to a foreign country in order to do research (say, for example, your novel is set in Ireland, but you have never been to Ireland, and an extended stay there would add authenticity to your story and to the dialect of your characters.)

Maybe we, as writers, can help each other through this difficult transition in publishing by helping to fund each other's campaigns.

I'm sure mine won't be anywhere as successful as Seth Godin's. But it doesn't have to be. If just 10 percent as successful, it would be a game-changing experience for me and my career.

III.

Before Your Book Publishes: The Planning Stages

THIRTY

Ten Sources to Spur Promotion Ideas

Anita Agers-Brooks

Authors are expected to do much of their own marketing. Been there, heard that—you can keep the t-shirt.

So what's a writer with little or no marketing experience to do? *Research.*

And get started early. Though my first book is almost a year from publication, I'm working on a Promotion Plan now. Naturally a strategic thinker, I'm thinking ahead. (If you haven't yet sold a project, this is prime brainstorming season.)

In a previous job, I worked sales and marketing for a clothing manufacturer, where my biggest account was Nike. They are marketing masters.

A minimum of eighteen months out, they plan the launch for any new apparel line. Nike knows the investment in time and energy pays back with interest. They study competitors. Survey customers. Review totally unrelated products. And sometimes, try things that fail.

But in the thinking stage, they don't toss any crazy idea.

As a new author, I don't have a mega-marketing budget like Nike. But their basic principles work with two hundred dollars like they do with two million.

Taking what I learned from past experience, here are ten sources I'm using to brainstorm a unique Book Promotion Plan:

1. **Read creative thinking books.** Some of my current faves are: *The $100 Startup, The Four-Hour Work Week, The Power of Full Engagement, The Well-Fed Writer, Red Hot Internet Publicity, The Wealthy Freelancer, Platform,* and *Shameless Self-Promotion and Networking for Christian Creatives.*

2. **Hunt for colorful partnering alternatives in the everyday.** Look around you with fresh eyes. Is there a marketing marriage in the making?

3. **Study other author websites for promotional ideas.** In the following examples, it's the concept, not necessarily the content, that interests me:

- Rise Again — The Novel
- Neil Gaiman
- Torry Martin
- The Cancer MD
- Author Media (Their marketing prowess rates high.)

4. **Observe projects, organizations, or businesses of different styles, to spark unique promotional ideas.** i.e. Concerts, chambers of commerce, beauty salons, amusement parks, hardware stores, talent shows, and more, are marketing fodder.

5. **Create a line of products to complement the book's message.** Brand image magnifies with diversity — and promotional products spread your message further.

6. **Target different personality types, genders, ages, and regions to reach a wider audience.** Never discount a potential demographic in the brainstorming phase.

7. **Ask for ideas.** Get your brave on. Ask the checkout person, waitress, plumber, even employees of places you visit on

vacation. They may offer fresh perspectives. But don't fail to tap into your professional networks as well.

8. **Help others with pure motives.** I believe we get what we honestly give.

9. **Stay true to the title.** I use this as an editing tool, but it works well with brand marketing also.

10. **Consult the Master Platform-Builder.** God constructs the sturdiest and sometimes strangest ways to display our messages. Trust Him to know the end in your beginning.

THIRTY-ONE

Seven No-Nonsense Book Launch Tips for Broke Authors

Gillian Marchenko

I am launching a book.

My memoir, *Sun Shine Down*, published at the end of August with T. S. Poetry Press. Eeek!

As a broke, green as the grass in mid-July first time author, I tackled the daunting assignment of launching a book like any other able-minded individual in North America.

I googled 'book launch.'

In .02 seconds, reputable, results-driven marketing and publicity firms jumped into my line of vision. These people surely could launch my book into the stratosphere!

But after some number crunching and a realistic talk with my husband about where hiring a publicist falls in the needs of a family of six (braces, soccer, therapy, FOOD), I conceded. We could not hire help for *Sun Shine Down*.

These days, whether we sign with a big publisher, a small press, or self-publish, we bear much of the responsibility for launching our own books. And it's hard work.

If you, too, are a broke new author, here are seven no-nonsense book-launching tips:

1) **Plan ahead**

If you wait to plan your book launch until your book is out, you're toast. Plan ahead. Start six months before you are to publish. Research, and consider elements of a book launch you will utilize.

2) Launch your book online

Social media is a marketing ocean. You've got Facebook, Twitter, Pinterest, Instagram . . . Where do you spend your time online? How can you introduce your book in those venues? With Amazon stomping on the book industry, it is a mistake not to market online.

3) Launch your book offline

Is a book party right for you? I'm hosting a party at a bar down the street from my house. I'm doing it on a Monday (because the venue is free then), providing appetizers, and using evites and Facebook events to publicize. **Extra tip:** Don't call your gathering a book signing. Call it a book party. Who doesn't love a good party?

4) Don't spam people to death with your book

Not everyone is excited to hear about your book all day every day. Post about your book (especially on your Author Fan Page–don't have one? Um, get going), but don't post several times a day. It just makes you look full of yourself. The trick is fun, cool content, and looking like you're not trying that hard even when you are.

4) Create a Facebook launch team

In an effort to build buzz about *Sun Shine Down*, I invited Facebook friends to join a super-secret launch group. I offered perks for joining (a free PDF advanced copy of the memoir, a thank-you on the blog, access to a secret group, and interaction with the author) and requirements (help promote for five weeks, post about the book on your blog, etc.). My secret group has been the highlight of promotion so far. Why? Because relationships are being strengthened and we are having fun! It is also a great way to ensure Amazon reviews once the book is published (make it a requirement).

5) **Get help!**

OK, I know that I sound like I am contradicting myself. But next time (God willing), I will hire someone or ask a friend to assist with some promotion. I'm talking about someone to help with a couple time-consuming tasks and who is affordable (as opposed to a publicist who would do everything and is expensive). I'm talking a flat rate per month to run a blog tour or help with the launch group. I'd like not to have that pressure, and I am finding out with this book that there are virtual assistants and others who could fit this description. *Note: I LOVE publicists, so If I get to that point in my career when I can hire one, I probably will.

6) **Create a new email address to send out official book launch news**

I simply created a new Gmail account with the name of my book and merged it with my current email account so that when I send out press releases and other book emails, it looks official (instead of the author sending them, which she is).

7) **Set expectations low**

This is my Eeyore personality coming out, but I suggest you set your expectations low. Then you'll be pleasantly surprised when something remarkable happens. Not an Eeyore? More a Tigger? OK, then expect like crazy. We are all different. In my experience, though, the people I thought would help publicize and raise excitement about *Sun Shine Down* haven't. I did have one or two wild cards, individuals I knew for a short time long ago who have become cheerleaders and promoters complete with pom-poms and cardboard signs.

Here's to successful book launches, and to many more hours with our butts in chairs, getting books written so that we can, gasp, go through the nonsense of launching again and again!

THIRTY-TWO

Marketing by the Dozen

Shellie Rushing Tomlinson

My next book, (which for our purposes here shall henceforth be spoken of as "The Faith Book" because it remains untitled)*, will release from Random House/Waterbrook early 2014. My dear editor, our own super agent Greg and his fantabulous wife, myself, and every friend and stranger I can pigeon-hole for a title discussion are in the throes of finding that elusive title. Oh, yes, I'm something of a bore about it. Feel free to run if you see me coming.

The mission is simple, and familiar to my fellow non-fiction authors. When my target audience sees this book on the shelves, he or she needs to connect with it, feel the need to purchase it, shove aside the huddled masses that have been awaiting its release, and hoof it to the checkout stand in record-setting speed. Whoa. I must have wandered into a daydream. Back to the real world and your regularly scheduled post.

The reality here is that "The Faith Book" will be vying for attention scraps among countless of those big-dog authors, not to mention scores of worthy books, new and old, from authors of every other genre, gracing the shelves. If funds allowed, and they don't, I would hire an outside publicist with the energy level of Richard Simmons and the marketing skills of whoever is behind Justin How-Did-That-Happen Bieber to beat the drum for it. Instead, I will send it out into the world and recommit to living by my own Happy Dozen Marketing Commandments:

1. I will help Waterbrook's in-house publicist to help me by remembering that I'm only one of many authors she has been assigned, and I will remind myself that any media contacts or leads I can gather or pass on to her will help maximize her time, and thus my book's exposure.

2. I will design and mail out postcards for "The Faith Book" to AT LEAST the bookstores that hosted signings for my last book and as many more as I possibly can.

3. I will maintain a current database of the stores that graciously welcome me in for a signing and I'll try to be prompt about following up with thank-you notes.

4. I will interact with the public as much as possible at book events and do my best to see each individual before me instead of a group. Everyone has a story and every event is an opportunity to capture new ones.

5. I will have material (bookmarks, business cards, etc.) to hand out at book signings so potential book buyers can feel comfortable walking away to consider the purchase instead of being put on the spot to purchase the book.

6. I will call radio stations and ask if they are interested in doing giveaways of my book and I'll consider it a good investment for the trade-off in airtime.

7. I will attend as many book festivals as physically possible to connect with readers and writers.

8. I will continue to make every effort to see that my weekly newsletter is entertaining and informative, keeping in mind that this is my way of giving back to the All Things Southern community (visit www.belleofallthingsouthern.com to find out more!).

9. I will not use social media selfishly. Communication, by definition, is a two-way street. My readers are people, not numbers, and they deserve to be treated as such.

10. I will support my fellow authors. (Towards that end: Dear author friends, please contact me if you would like to guest on my blog at All Things Southern.)

11. I will do readings at area libraries. Their patrons may not buy books, but they are readers. As writers we have a shared responsibility to promote reading.

And number twelve of my Happy Dozen:

12. I will enjoy my life while I'm promoting my work, knowing that I am living what I first dreamed many years ago as a little girl perched in the top of my reading/writing mimosa tree. I am a writer and I will be grateful for that privilege.

*Shellie did eventually come up with a title for that book—it's called *Heart Wide Open: Trading Mundane Faith for an Exuberant Life with Jesus.* It published in March 2014.

THIRTY-THREE

The Juggling Act of Marketing While You Write

Anita Agers-Brooks

I learned a lot from the publication and release of my first book. Instead of dwelling on what I did wrong or inefficiently, I'm focusing on improving those areas when *Getting Through What You Can't Get Over* releases in April via Barbour Publishing.

For instance, while writing my first release, if I had known then what I know now, I wouldn't have held my enthusiasm back. I would have let my natural flow of excitement transfer into some of my Tweets, Facebook posts, LinkedIn shares, and Pinterest pins. I wouldn't have sold to people, but would have offered a few teasers, a new sentence, a punchy line taken from my project, while I was writing it, getting people interested early. Word of mouth is still the best marketing vehicle around.

I would have blogged about the process more. (Something I just started doing on my Writing Wednesday posts at anitabrooks.com.)

I would have posted a few videos on YouTube about struggles, victories, disappointments, encouragements, life interruptions, cave-dwellings, along with other writing downs and ups. Adding more visual author media to marketing efforts enhances the experience for readers. This allows audiences to read tone of voice, facial expressions, and body language, as well as words.

I would have listened to Michael Hyatt's fantastic audio series, *Get Published*, while I was writing, not shortly after my book released. Then I would have acted on many of his insider suggestions.

While I juggle writing, marketing my current book, pre-release marketing for my new one, family, friends, speaking, coaching, and the occasional unexpected crisis, I'm also celebrating a few things I did right on the first go around.

I made new connections, and built some solid and life-long relationships with people who can benefit my writing career, but more importantly, are now my friends. We help each other, encourage, pray, and genuinely care about what happens to each other, more than we care about what happens with our careers.

I proved myself capable as a professional writer and marketer. Building credibility and practicing integrity at the foundation of your career provides a solid footing to propel you forward as you move ahead with new books, articles, and posts. I see myself as a slow and steady author, who will win the race through consistency and solid growth. I'd rather experience longevity, versus a fast start that sputters in a flash.

I made some marketing mistakes, but didn't let them become catalysts for giving up. Instead, I evaluated where things fell apart, and used those insights to make informed decisions and new plans. Some things I need to cut out completely, but most only require a few tweaks, and my updated marketing plans will prove more profitable.

But the most powerful thing I did right the first time, and am continuing to do now, is this: I am not leaning on my own understanding. Instead, I am asking God where to invest my talents. Who are the readers? Where should I market? What is the best use of my energy? When should I time marketing efforts? How should I balance the juggling act of marketing while I write?

In the end, none of us knows the perfect marketing plan. But, those who succeed exhibit similar qualities. Guts, consistency, resolve, humility, a teachable spirit, listening ears, watching eyes, and a quitting-is-not-an-option determination. No matter how much juggling is required.

THIRTY-FOUR

How to Create an Author Press Kit

Julie Cantrell

One of the most effective strategies for book marketing is to create a **press kit**. This costs no money, but it's a worthwhile investment of time because the kit will be used from pre-launch throughout the full life of the book.

WHAT IS AN AUTHOR PRESS KIT?

A well-designed author press kit serves as an easy-to-read source of information about a particular book. The goal is to convince folks to read this book and to share it with others.

Of course, the author's unique skills should be highlighted as well, because media outlets need a reason to interview an author OTHER THAN the fact that their book is for sale. In other words, what makes THIS particular author worthy of air time/ink/review/shelf space?

WHO READS THE PRESS KIT?

The kit should be designed to reach:

- Book clubs
- Booksellers
- Print and online editors (magazines, newspapers, review sites, etc.)
- Media outlets and journalists (print, radio, web, podcast, etc.)

- Librarians
- Readers (as far reaching as possible but target specific readership)
- Reviewers (both professional and arm chair)
- And anyone interested in the work

With millions of books on shelves/cybershelves, the kit must convince people to choose THIS ONE.

HOW TO CREATE AN AUTHOR PRESS KIT:

An author press kit consists of five components.

- **Cover Art:** A high resolution jpg of the book's cover.
- **Sell Sheet:** A quick list of the book's publishing information. Include back-cover copy, the specific editions of the book and availability; date of publication; name of publisher; and a general scope of the marketing/promotion plan (regional vs. national tour, blog tour, media interviews, advertising campaign, publicist, etc.). Give folks an idea of how much effort is being put into this campaign and be sure to include contact information for author and/or publicist.
- **Press Release:** This serves as the official press release for the book. Follow the traditional format and exhibit professional know-how.
- **Interview Q&A:** Provide a sample interview. Let this show the author's personality, interesting background, or special skills. Offer something unique that would engage listeners/readers.
- **Sample Chapters:** Link to a free chapter or two on Scribd. Offer a sneak peek that showcases the author's talent and the tone of the book.

HOW TO SHARE THE PRESS KIT:

Once the kit is complete, convert it to PDFs and organize a PRESS KIT folder.

- Upload PDFs to an author website for easy download.
- Before launch, research bloggers, media outlets, libraries, booksellers, book clubs, etc. and create spreadsheets for each. Send email or postcards to these targets inviting them to download a free author press kit with sample chapters of the soon-to-be-released book.
- Also share links via social media and other sites geared toward reaching readers.

With a little effort, a proper press kit can impress and intrigue. If done right, the kit will lead folks to a new book before it ever hits shelves.

THIRTY-FIVE

Keeping Track of Contacts, Media History, and Speaking Engagements

Rachel Randolph

Many of us creative types wish to not be bothered with anything but our *craft*, especially when a deadline is approaching. But as your electric company has probably conveyed to you, creative types aren't exempt from pesky little tasks like paying bills, and the IRS doesn't excuse us from keeping up with our receipts and paperwork either. Much the same, our publishers need their right-brained authors to tap into that left hemisphere on occasion.

Last week, my co-author/mom and I worked on our publisher's Advanced Sales and Marketing Information (ASMI), which included compiling a list of influencers that should receive a copy of the book. Our book deadline is still three months away and it won't be on the shelves for another year. As a newbie author I didn't know to plan for this project and my experienced co-author was surprised at how early it was being requested. It seems we authors have driven our publishers to request the information earlier and earlier.

If you've thought ahead and kept good records, the gathering of information will not be a big deal. Then, you can focus on the fun part of the ASMI, the description of your book, the key take-aways, the reason you're writing it and so on. If you haven't kept good records, though, you will likely spend days tracking down addresses and contacts, finding the best full-service moving rates at www.fullservicemovers.biz and racking your brain to remember the name of the church where you spoke in the Fall of 2005 and what the call letters are for that radio station in Milwaukee that interviewed you last spring.

Don't be surprised when you are frantically trying to meet your deadline and your publisher says, "Oh, by the way, we need the following in three weeks."

A list of names, professional titles, and addresses of 50 influential people who can be counted on to help promote your book.

As someone who has done this legwork for self-published authors, I can say that you really want to take advantage of this offer. It's a lot of work and expensive to package and mail 50 or more books. Your publisher is offering, but you need the connections and their contact information. In the day of email and Facebook, unless you run a business, it's rare to exchange physical addresses. I suggest, as you meet potential influencers, to tell them you are writing a book and would love their address so you can have a copy sent to them when it comes out (you don't have to have a contract to use this line). When you get an address, quickly add it to your online contact database and tag the person as a potential influencer. Excel is an excellent and easy place to track contacts.

A list of prominent people from whom we should request an endorsement.

If you are lucky or have put in the time to network with other authors or experts in your field, you might know a few prominent people who would gladly write an endorsement for you. Even if you don't know a person, if they would be a perfect endorser for your book and you can get their address, include them. You may be surprised who will say yes. One of my self-publishing clients requested an endorsement from Olivia-Newton John on her book *Alphatudes: The Alphabet of Gratitude.* Instead of an endorsement, Olivia ended up offering a free download of her song "Grace and Gratitude" with the purchase of the book. Start a contact record for any potential endorser now or when you are researching competition for your proposal. Those "competitors" may be perfect people to ask.

A list of media you think should receive a copy of the book.

Your publisher will have a set of media contacts that they already plan to send your book to, but you can't rely on them to know every local or topic-specific outlet. The great news is they will ask you for your input on this, since you know your topic best. As you come across media outlets (blogs, magazines, newspapers, television shows) that would be perfect for your book, put their mailing information in your database.

A list of your previous media and speaking history.

For some, this may be a short and easy list. My writing and speaking career is just getting started, so I I've had very few media and speaking appearances, and even still, I almost forgot some of the details I needed.

My mom, on the other hand, has been writing and speaking for almost two decades. Try remembering 20 years of speaking engagements and interviews for 40-plus books. My suggestion is to keep one ongoing spreadsheet for speeches and one for media. Every time you finish an interview or publish an article, write down all the details. The name of your contact person, the host's name, the topic, the date, etc. Put contact information in your contact database, though, not on these forms, so you only have to keep one record updated

Keeping track of all your speeches in one place will not only make it easier to fill out your ASMI, but will also give you a quick, sortable history when you need a reference for a certain speaking topic or want to pitch something fresh to a previous client.

As excited as you might be for your first few interviews, you'd be surprised how quickly you'll forget which magazine interviewed you on what topic or which TV producer you worked with. Keep it all in one place with an easy spreadsheet.

THIRTY-SIX

Celebrate with a Launch Party

Julie Cantrell

When my debut novel hit shelves, I wanted to do something special. Too many people in my community had played a part in the journey, and I wanted everyone involved to be publicly acknowledged for their contributions to the book.

The night before the official release date, we held a Launch Party at our local bookstore, Square Books. I didn't have a big budget, so we served champagne and chocolate to keep the event nice but affordable. (We also provided non-alcoholic bubbly so everyone could participate in the toast.) The night was lovely. Beyond lovely. And it will always be a favorite memory of mine.

If you're thinking of having a launch party, and I strongly encourage you to do so, keep these simple tips in mind when planning your big event.

1. **Consider your crowd.** Ours is a laid-back group from all walks of life, so I wanted everyone to feel comfortable. We kept it very low key and emphasized the "come as you are, bring the kids" aspect of the evening. The public was invited.

2. **Consider your space.** Our bookstore hosts many author events each month and is prepared for such crowds. It's always great to support a local bookseller, but if you don't have access to such a store/gift shop, think of themes that correspond with your book (knitting, outdoors, swimming, cooking, etc.) and tie the launch party into a suitable location.

3. **Consider your time.** A typical schedule is to have a "soft start." Allow folks to trickle in and mingle, enjoying the free refreshments while you chat and sign a few copies to get the evening going. Then the bookseller (host) introduces you, and you speak for approximately 20 minutes. Then, you sign again.

4. **Consider your speech.** It's best to mix up your presentation with a little reading, telling how the book came to be, thanking folks involved, and . . . if appropriate . . . inserting some sort of entertainment. I had two singers perform one song each to give voice to two of my favorite characters. Both gave emotional performances that moved many to tears, and I think it was the best part of the night.

5. **Consider your signature.** I admit I have AWFUL penmanship, but I do plan ahead and bring a stash of good pens. Always a good idea.

You'll probably be too busy to think about taking pictures, so ask a friend to capture the night on film. Believe me, it'll all be a blur. And don't forget the minor details: wine glasses, champagne flutes, bottle openers, cake knife, napkins, plates, utensils, tablecloth, camera, extra books, bookmarks, etc.

Finally, if you plan to sell books at the launch, I strongly recommend you let someone else handle the sales. The last thing you want to worry about is money. It's a once in a lifetime moment. Live it up!

THIRTY-SEVEN

Planning a Book Release Party

Kariss Lynch

I've said it once and I'll say it again, an author does much more than just write. In fact, understanding this was my biggest learning curve once I penned my John Hancock on my first contract. You are a writer, editor, marketer, publicist, your own biggest cheerleader, and your own worst critic. Not to mention the fact that you have multiple voices talking to you at one time as you write. Don't worry . . . that's normal. Kind of.

This year, I added "party planner" to my growing writing resume as I prepared for the release of *Shadowed* just two short months ago. When *Shaken* released in 2014, my friends planned a sweet party to celebrate. This year, it was my turn to grab the wheel. Only I had no idea where to begin! But like all things in this writing journey, the learning curve is steep, the lessons memorable, and the end result rewarding.

The release party doesn't have to be stressful! Here are some tips I picked up along the way.

1. <u>Choose a theme</u>.

I planned two different parties with the help of loved ones. I wanted to theme the parties, so I selected decorations and small touches according to the audience. Since some of the major moments in *Shadowed* are centered around sunsets and the ocean and an opening scene with fireworks, I found decorations that flowed like water and paper décor that resembled the pop of color bursting in a dark sky. It was a fun way to set the stage. For the second party, we decided to go with simple and elegant to fit the audience coming. We chose a room lined with windows overlooking downtown, decorated a center table with roses, set up a sidebar with refreshments, and left an open space for mingling and signing books.

2. <u>Delegate the details</u>.

I still didn't pull this off on my own. In fact, I had a moment where I almost threw in the towel. But friends and family came to the rescue. Friends volunteered to bring refreshments and plastic ware that fit the beach theme. Others donated door prizes like Fossil watches and a hand-lettered quote from *Shadowed* framed beautifully. Another friend set up a photo booth complete with reading glasses and chalkboards that represented different plot twists. Party-goers could grab their favorite pair of reading glasses, a chalkboard with their favorite plot twist, and enact the scene on camera.

3. <u>Send the invite</u>.

Gather those around you who weathered the journey with you. Those who sat through the tears and endless plot conversations, the ones who left meals on your doorstep, or talked you off the ledge when you wanted to quit. Let them celebrate this win with you! As excited as your readers will be, these people will be even more excited for you, and let's be honest, you couldn't have reached this accomplishment without them. Then, encourage them to bring their friends, friends who may just be curious about you as an author, who may just want to come for the party, and who may just walk away as fans of your work. Use Facebook or Evite to send a mass message so that folks can easily respond

4. <u>Remember the journey</u>.

Don't forget to hit pause in the craziness and excitement and remember. Remember from whence you've come. Remember the winding road that led you to this point, the road that seemed to never end and had too many bumps to identify. Remember that writing is your calling. Remember the One who gave you the story in the first place.

5. <u>Celebrate</u>!

Bask in the joy of completion, of your baby entering the wide, wide world. Ask a couple of your confidants to keep an eye on the refreshments and remind people to turn in their tickets for door prizes, then cut loose and celebrate. Share your heart, speak of the journey, talk about the story, smile, laugh, sell books, giveaway a few, and praise God for the gift of completion, of release day, and all He taught you along the way.

When all is said and done, clean up, sleep up, then hit the desk. You've got another manuscript to finish.

THIRTY-EIGHT

Launching Your Book with Power

The Writing Sisters, Betsy Duffey and Laurie Myers

How do you launch a book with power?

When we neared the launch date for our book, *The Shepherd's Song*, we began to become anxious. Pressure built. How could be good stewards of this book that we felt God had place in our hands? What to do? We read, we googled, we asked our friends, but nothing seemed quite right. Then, we remembered.

The basis of the book had been prayer. We had prayed together during the writing of the book. We had prayed for each other and we had enlisted a prayer team to pray. The answer was simple. We would launch the book with prayer. But how?

Forty days out from the release of the book we began a forty-day prayer launch. We prayed first for God to give us 40 people who would pray for 40 days. We put the request out on social media and we had 164 people sign up to pray with us. God blessed us abundantly.

This is how we set it up:

We created a list on Mail Chimp with a sign-up form that we posted on Twitter and Facebook and sent out to our newsletter list. It was a simple request for anyone who wanted to join the prayer launch for the book.

We sent a one-sentence email prayer by Mail Chimp to the 164 people each morning for 40 days. Like these short prayers:

Put this book in the right hands at the right times.
Prepare the hearts of the people in Germany for this book.
Bless the marketing team as they plan for this book.
Bless the readers to accept God as their Shepherd.

For 40 days we all prayed. Then the book went out!

So, how do you evaluate the success of a prayer launch? You can't measure the results in numbers. But here are some things that happened afterwards.

During an event at a church in South Carolina a woman we did not know came up and introduced herself. She said, "I prayed for this book." A few tears were shed!

A woman in North Carolina was one of our first reviewers on Amazon. Her life had been changed by the book as she prayed for others to be moved by God's Word.

Several of the prayer partners wrote to tell how the daily prayers had been used by God in their own lives on a particular day.

Best of all we were reminded daily that the book was God's and not ours. That He would use His ways to share His words. That we had no need to be anxious.

IV.

Harnessing Social Media to Sell Books

THIRTY-NINE

DIY: Step-by-Step Guide to Making a Book Trailer

Julie Cantrell

What is a Book Trailer?
A book trailer is a brief video used to market a book. Like a trailer for a motion picture, book trailers can make your title stand out among the masses.

Many professionals will produce trailers for a hefty fee, but why not do it yourself?

Four Simple Tools

1. Computer: The first thing you need is a PC or MAC with decent operating speed. We used a PC with Windows 7. Older versions of Windows may be slow to process video data.

2. Camera: Recording in high definition (HD) is not necessary for posting on websites like YouTube. We used a digital SLR camera (Canon EOS Rebel T2i), but we did not film in HD. Instead, we used 640 x 480 pixels which created a much more manageable file size. (TIP: Make sure your software will open your video file type before you shoot the trailer.)

3. Tripod: This is a must. Use a tripod. Always.

4. Microphones: If you plan to include external sounds/voices, use microphones.

Five Steps and You're Done!

1. Setting: Choose locations based on your book's theme. Obtain permission to film on anyone else's property, and do not show anyone in the film without their permission (this includes folks in the background).

2. Shooting: Shoot short segments and paste them together using a video software package. We used Windows Live Movie Maker which was easy to use and comes with Windows 7.

3. Editing: Transfer all the video segments into a single folder on your computer. Decide on the order of the videos in advance (ex: save as Trailer1, Trailer2, etc.). Begin inserting them into the software and trim as needed. You can use the audio from the original film segments or block it out completely and use a separate audio file.

4. Adding Music: While some royalty-free music is available online, my teen daughter composed the music for our trailer. She performed it on our piano, and we recorded it using Microsoft Sound Recorder on our laptop (which is equipped with a built-in microphone). This program is on all Windows computers.

5. Polishing: Your publisher may be willing to add a little polish and a company logo. If so, the best way to share video file access with another editor is to use Dropbox.

Share the Love

Finally, save the file to a common format (MPEG-4 or AVI) or upload directly to YouTube from your software. From YouTube, I embedded my trailer on my website, added it to my author profiles on sites like Barnes & Noble and Goodreads, and shared it with friends through my blogsite. To post on Amazon,

SheWrites and others, you need a direct file (not the YouTube upload). Many authors include a link to the trailer in their press kit, and some even distribute DVDs to local booksellers.

Have fun, and come back to share your trailer with us here at the Cooler!

If you don't have the desire to take on the challenge of creating a trailer yourself, here are a few professionals who create book trailers:

Pulse Point Design (www.pulsepointdesign.com)

Bemis Promotions (www.bemispromotions.com)

Oh, and once you have a book trailer, do your research and take the time to upload your trailer onto your website and/or blog as well as the many different sites available to help promote it, such as: Amazon.com, Youtube.com, and Tangle.com.

FORTY

How to Create a Free E-Book for Your Website

Melissa K. Norris

People love to receive stuff for free. Ever wandered through Costco in the afternoon? You can always spot the free sample stands by the crowds gathered 'round.

Our readers are no different. They love to get stuff for free, and what better way to encourage or thank them for signing up to your blog posts than with a free e-book?

You may be unsure what content to include in your e-book. Ask your readers. I put a poll on my website asking what subject people would like to see more. This helped me decide what to write my e-book about. Take a look at your web stats; which posts have the highest views?

Once you've decided on your topic, start writing it. Keep it on the shorter side; it doesn't need to be a full book length. Under five thousand words is a good guideline. Remember to offer new content in your book. Because it's electronic, you can and should link to articles on your blog for further reading and value to the reader.

After your e-book is finished, save it as a PDF file and then upload it to your website. Keep it unassigned (for self-hosted WordPress) and copy the location.

I use Feedburner as my RSS and email subscription service for my website. I downloaded my existing email subscribers addresses to MailChimp and sent them out a free copy thanking them for being with me. You never want to forget your current readers in the search for new ones.

For new subscribers, I included the PDF link in the email they receive from Feedburner when they sign up for my blog. This allowed for free automation and instant access for the reader.

If you use Feedburner and have a sign-up box on your website, I highly recommend customizing the sign-up box. Even if you don't have an e-book to offer yet, you should list the benefits subscribers receive when they sign up for your emails.

By using the Feedburner verification email to send out my free e-book link, I realize people don't have to verify in order to get the free copy. But if they don't like my free e-book and choose not to verify to get my posts, then they most likely would have unsubscribed anyway.

FORTY-ONE

Does Free Really Help Sell Books?

Melissa K. Norris

As I've been working on the launch of my new book, I'm struggling with how much to give away for free. I've read conflicting reports on offering your book without cost.

Some say you'll gain so much word of mouth that we all should do it. Others say you devalue your content and make those who have paid for it feel cheated.

What is an author to do?

My new book launches today.

To help promote it, I decided to give something away for free and a bonus gift. But I put a time limit on it. If I know I've got a limited time frame it makes me get to it first. I'm thinking I can't be the only one who thinks this way.

I'm offering up my first chapter for free. Now that's nothing new, you say. Authors do this all over the place.

But not all authors use this great free application called "Pay with a Tweet." In order to read my first chapter, people can choose to pay with a tweet or Facebook share. It represents word-of-mouth marketing for me and also gives the reader something for free.

That's not my only freebie. For every reader who purchases my book on Amazon and forwards me the copy of their proof of purchase, email, and mailing address, I'm going to mail them a secret recipe and the link to a full-length bonus chapter—but only through the end of this month.

I'm hoping this will help people to purchase now, before it falls onto their to-do list and is forgotten. I also feel that these items provide real value and content to the readers of my book. Because that's what great marketing boils down to: the reader asking, what's in it for me?

FORTY-TWO

How to Stage an Online Blitz

Jan Dunlap

After spending five days eating, drinking, and sleeping (well, maybe not so much sleeping as lying awake with the brain on overload) the promotion of my free Kindle download last week, I've come up with what I call 'Jan's **TIP**' for any writer planning a similar online marketing blitz.

T is for Timing.

Choose your **campaign dates** carefully. My book, *A Murder of Crows*, takes place in October and opens with a scarecrow display; picking an October date for the promotion was an easy choice. It also afforded me lots of tie-in opportunities: I could mention the book in response to any blog, Facebook or Pinterest item that was about Halloween or scarecrows. Think seasonally!

Timing is also about **when you post** on social networks. I read blogs on Social Media Examiner and subscribe to Rob Eager's marketing posts, and I've learned the best days and times to post to get the most fan engagement: Wednesday through Sunday. I kicked off my promotion with announcements on Sunday and pushed hard with posts Thursday and Friday.

Finally, timing is about you, and **how much time you can devote** to managing your promotional campaign. I spent at least four to five hours a day online posting, emailing, commenting on blogs, updating lists of contacts and prospecting for new ones. I spent two more hours each day strategizing what to do the next day, exploring new markets and tracking sales/download data. If you want to run a successful campaign, it's a full-time job!

I is for Images.

Research has shown that **images are the keys to social network sharing**. To keep posts fresh and continually attention-grabbing, you need to switch up the images you post. I developed six images to use during my five days of promotion, and changed the images I posted every day, with different short text messages. By the end of the week, I'd seen all six images reposted on different networks. It kept my message alive in the universe of Facebook and Pinterest, where the typical 'life' of a post is only three hours.

P is for Preparation.

I spent weeks—years, actually—preparing. I made solid **contacts in my target audiences** over the last few years and asked for book reviews and assistance in promoting my free Kindle deal. I put together **a team** of fans, reviewers, bloggers, and key influencers to help me focus on getting the word out the week of the promotion, and supplied them with my **prepared images and text** to use on their own networks. My **list of websites and FB pages** to contact during my promotion week numbered over 100 (and in the course of the week, it continued to grow as I stumbled on new connections—which are now part of my data base for future book promotion).

So that's 'Jan's **TIP**.' Take it for what it's worth. For me, it was worth around 4000 Kindle downloads in five days . . . and a bump in the sales of other books in my series.

FORTY-THREE

How I Boosted My Book to 30x More People

Jan Dunlap

I finally bit the bullet. I boosted a post on Facebook.

For years, I've seen that annoying little message you get on your author page about paying to boost your posts. Because I'm cheap (and still suspicious of social media's REAL intent, i.e. who needs to know what I buy, who I connect with, and what I like? Creepy . . .), I refused to give it a try. If my books can't make it on their own merits, so be it—I'll be content with small audiences, extremely limited financial reward, and the personal gratification that I haven't caved to crass commercialism.

And then last month after I started getting consistent raves about my new thriller "Heaven's Gate," I thought, "What the heck. It's only $20."

Actually, it ended up being $60, since I decided if I was going to experiment, I wanted to see what a week of boosted posts could do rather than one day, which is what $20 will buy. Knowing that most buyers need to be exposed to a product seven times before they buy (have you heard of the Rule of Seven?), I figured one day of boosting was throwing away cash, but seven days might just convert into some sales. I can now tell you, without reservation, that $60 worth of boosting on Facebook can go a long way in giving your book exposure and building your audience, and now I can't wait to give my other books the same treatment.

Here are the numbers from my week-long experiment:

1. Organic reach peaked at 305 on Day 7, while paid reach was 9045. That's **30x more people** reached than my normal posting! Not only that, but thanks to my OCD tendencies, I checked one last time on Day 10 (remember I only paid for 7 days of boosting) and was happy to see a new total of 9432. **The post was still being shared after my paid boosting**! Score!

2. I monitored my book's print and e-book rankings on my amazon Author Central page (you do have one of these, right?) for the boosting's duration. By Day 6, my e-book ranking had reached 924 in the Paranormal category after starting on Day 1 at 3366; the biggest jump was from Day 1 to Day 2, which tells me that first burst of posting **made an impact that powered the rest of the week**. Recalling the Rule of Seven and the impact of repeated impressions, though, I looked again on Day 18, only to find my e-book ranking better than ever at 831!

3. As for print, my book moved from its initial 76,331 ranking to 8535 on Day 5. Clearly, somebody was paying attention.

Even knowing that rankings are a superficial measure (rankings don't equal sale units), I decided that post boosting may not be such a bad idea for marketing after all. While the actual sales numbers are still in question, I know for a fact that more people have seen my book's cover thanks to post boosting than would have otherwise. And that's one step closer to buying my book.

FORTY-FOUR

10 Tips for Converting Website Visitors to Customers

Janalyn Voigt

The thing I still grapple with is turning website visits into sales—any advice on that piece?

This question to a post I wrote, "Drive Traffic to Your Website or Social Media Sites (7 Things a Writer Should Know)," inspired today's topic. Driving paying customers to your website is only a matter of outlining and implementing the steps to take. Here are some things to consider.

1. **Make it professional and appealing.** If your website is garish, disorganized, or amateurish, revamp it before inviting company over.

2. **Blog for your target audience.** Not everyone should blog, but if the idea appeals to you, ask yourself who will come to your site. What would draw them and make them come back? To reach more people, you might want to consider other blogging formats like photoblogging, vlogging (videos), and podcasts in addition to text.

3. **Keep an email list** and notify it of new blog posts. You can include a purchase offer with a call to action at the

end of each of your posts. This is especially effective because research suggests people most often respond to a product with a purchase after seven offers.

4. **Offer an email newsletter.** This is one of the best ways to keep in touch with customers on an ongoing basis. Each time your newsletter shows up in their email inboxes, you and your product(s) will come to mind. This makes you part of the fabric of their everyday lives.

5. **Engage readers.** Answer their questions, host a forum, offer samples of your writing. Anything goes, just so long as you entertain readers while remaining consistent with your brand. If you're stuck for ideas, get together with a friend or friends and brainstorm.

6. **Host a contest** to draw readers. Give away something of value and require email signup for entry. When your site gains page rank, you'll likely receive offers of free products in exchange for promoting them. You can also sign up for affiliations that allow you to distribute sample products. As an example, during a blog parade I gave away a complimentary copy of scrapbooking software.

7. **Launch an ongoing giveaway** in exchange for email list sign up. Giving away products when you're trying to make money may seem counterintuitive, but offering something of value for free can more readily put you in the position of a trusted mentor to visitors. Remember that people buy from those they like and trust and who care about them. False motives stand out and won't earn you sales. Be genuine and speak from your passions. Giveaways don't have to be published books. Use your creativity to come up with ideas. Lists and reports have a high perceived value. Whatever you give away,

let it come from you. On my Live Write Breathe site (www.livewritebreathe.com) for writers, I give away free letterhead stationery and a query letter template that I designed. Since photography is one of my hobbies, at NovelBooks.org, where I inform readers about wholesome books and authors, I offer free computer wallpaper and an additional chance to win book giveaways for email sign up.

8. **Offer a quality product or products.** This should go without saying. If you want the best results for your efforts, be generous.

9. **Include a landing page** with value for the reader and a single call to action. Resist the urge to bore visitors by making your landing page a site directory. That's what your navigation menu is for. Instead, determine what you want to gain and ask for it in a clear appeal. What if you want more than one thing? Combine them. (Purchase an autographed copy of my latest book, *How Penguins Waddle*, and receive a free copy of my in-depth report on water birds. As a special bonus, you'll also receive the monthly Antarctic Adventure newsletter.) It's all about presentation.

10. **Promote.** Drive traffic to your site by making informed comments (but not blatant self-promotion) on forums and sites with an audience similar to your own. Cross-promoting with another writer or business can also be effective. You should update your social networks with links to your sites and a catchy blurb or excerpt.

Most writers, being artists, can feel a little challenged when it comes to setting up shop. Converting website traffic to sales is what we have to do, though, to reach and retain readers.

FORTY-FIVE

Six Things Writers Need to Know About Email Marketing

Jordyn Redwood

Not long ago I was ~~procrastinating my writing duties~~ perusing Facebook and a fellow author (whom I know and love and who therefore will remain anonymous) was spouting off about how much she hates to get emails without her permission. "This is illegal!" she cried (as much as you can cry out on Facebook, the land of the overused exclamation point.) Many people commented their mutual disgust.

I, however, did not. You see, I've had a lot of personal experience with this lately and I thought I'd share what I learned with you.

Recently, I started working for a faith-based website. We wanted a large email campaign to build awareness. We hired a company to help us achieve this goal. For our target list, we researched *public* information. We didn't use a computer software program or other nefarious means to gather info, but when we started to send e-mails through this company, we got the red light. The question became: How did you collect email addresses? We disclosed that it was through public information on the web.

This company wanted a permission-based email list in order to allow us to use their services. This could be achieved either through a personal phone call or the interested party filling out a web-based contact form. This is how subscription-based email systems like Mail Chimp work. You fill out a contact form and the author then has permission to e-mail you.

Everyone stays out of trouble.

The company I work for soon became familiar with the CAN-SPAM Act of 2003.

In short, you can email someone without their permission but that email needs to meet VERY specific requirements. Using an e-mail service like Mail Chimp accomplishes this and is likely why authors prefer it. However, you might need to email some-one without "express consent" in order to see if they want to further know about your product.

E-mail services look at bounce rates. A bounce rate greater than the industry standard of 5 percent indicates the sender may be using substandard means to gather email addresses. Some of these means include using a computer program, guessing what the email address might be, and (according to this company) re-searching *public sources*.

But say you've had a reader contact you and you want to see if they'll sign up for your newsletter. They haven't given you "express consent" to email them (or advertise to them) but you think they might be interested in some of your product because they sent you a nice letter. You could send them an email asking them to sign up for your newsletter. In order to be in compli-ance with the law, that email would need to meet these require-ments. I'll be paraphrasing somewhat.

1. You must clearly identify who is sending the e-mail.
2. Use forthright subject lines. *"Request to sign up for my newsletter!"*
3. If the message is an ad, it must be clearly stated.

4. There must be a physical address in the body of the e-mail for you or the business. As an author, I wouldn't suggest using your personal address. Get a PO box.

5. Tell recipients how they can opt out and then honor their requests within 10 business days. *"If you'd like to stop getting these e-mails– please reply with STOP."*

6. If you're using a company, they need to be following these rules as well.

So, technically, you can "cold email" someone, but you'll need to hit these points. If you don't, it can result in hefty fines. If you choose to not use a subscription based email service to build your newsletter list (which I do recommend), then read up on this law and (because I'm not a lawyer) consult a lawyer if you have additional questions.

FORTY-SIX

How I Discover New Books—
Hint, Not in a Bookstore

Jordyn Redwood

It's been said that the reason an author should stick to traditional publishing is book discoverability and distribution by way of a publisher's marketing budget and sales staff.

I was fortunate to get a three-book deal with a mid-size Christian publisher who did get behind my book generously with marketing dollars. They even landed me in Sam's Club with my first two books in hundreds of stores nationwide.

Just, why, didn't I hit the bestseller lists? I think the books are good. *Proof* and *Poison* got starred reviews from *Library Journal*. Both were nominated (though never won) for awards. Lots of favorable reviews.

In fact, I might even say that landing in Sam's Club hurt me a little. Why? The issue with Sam's club is it's a BIG order. It's a risk for the publisher. If you're not a well-known name who can move those novels many are going to get returned and your royalty report is going to look like a defaulted home loan and the bank is knocking on your door.

I began to analyze how I discover books, and does it match with the way a traditional publisher markets novels?

Sure, your best chance of getting into a bookstore is partnering with a traditional publisher, but how often are you going to bookstores anymore? I used to go weekly, when they were close. There aren't any close ones anymore. The one at the mall I would stop in while shopping for other things . . . gone . . . both of them. The closest bookstore is a 15-20-minute drive. And as NYT-bestselling author Jamie McGuire has blogged about, even she wasn't seeing her novels in bookstores during release week.

Here is a list of how I now discover books.

1. <u>Goodreads Reviews</u>. Goodreads is the place for people who LOVE books and where book lovers leave reviews. I find I have more Goodreads reviews than Amazon reviews. I have close to 2,500 friends on Goodreads. Every day, I get an e-mail of their reviews. I've come to know whose reading tastes are similar to mine. A good review of a book will cause me to look further on Amazon. Plus, since I'm friends with so many, I get exposed to a wide variety of books outside my general reading genre (suspense) that I probably wouldn't have heard about— even browsing bookstore aisles.

2. <u>Amazon Lists</u>. Amazon lists are fun to browse. Of course, there is always the 100 top paid and free Kindle lists, but I also look at genre-specific top 100 lists. I also pay attention to novels getting a crazy number of reviews and try and read those to see what is catching the reader's eye. So, from my first two examples, I don't think any author can say that reviews don't matter . . . they do.

3. <u>Advertising Lists</u>. There are a couple of advertising lists that I belong to—BookBub and Inspired Reads. On these sites, you can narrow down the types of e-mails you receive to genres you like. Every day you'll get an e-mail about books that are on sale. Bookbub lists are the primary way I'm *buying* books. If I see an interesting book cover then I click the buy link for Amazon and check out reviews. Based on the number of reviews, I make

a decision about whether or not to buy the novel. BookBub has a very good reputation among authors that, though pricey, is generally a good investment of your marketing dollars. I think the same is true with Inspired Reads for their reach/price ratio.

4. <u>Word of Mouth</u>. I'm like every other human being. If a good friend says, "You must read this book," it will climb up to the top of my TBR list. The more people that say it—the more likely I am to read it. One author I'd almost given up on until a good friend said, "Just read this one. If you don't like it, I give you permission to never read this author again." Reading that novel changed my opinion of the author and their work.

What I find is that I'm rarely in a bookstore anymore but I'm discovering a lot more books because these things are available to me every day.

For my fall release, this is how I'm spending my marketing money. I'll likely not be arranging bookstore book signings, but that's a topic for another time.

V.

After Your Book Publishes: Staying Enthusiastic and Creative

FORTY-SEVEN

The Splash-Launch vs. the Slow Build

J. Parker

My new book, *Hot, Holy, and Humorous: Sex in Marriage by God's Design*, released the same week that my oldest son graduated from high school. Although I was excited to finally see my book out, this was not excellent timing for me and my family.

Consequently, I didn't do a lot on day one, day two, or even a few days after the release to promote my book. I was too busy pulling together the final details of the cap-and-gown experience for my son. The way I figured, I'd spent a few years working on my book, but eighteen years working on the kid – so the latter won out.

But all that is okay, because I'm not a big believer in the splash-launch. Not that I'm against it in the least! It's wonderful when a much-anticipated book hits the shelves with well-deserved fanfare. Seriously, a book is not easy to birth, so cue the fireworks! However, a big splash isn't what really matters for the long-term success of a book.

In the music world, we all know about the one-hit wonders who burst forth on the scene with as much hoopla as Mardi Gras in New Orleans. And then ... they were gone. Sure, the splash rippled outward, but eventually the waters calmed.

Meanwhile, Aerosmith's first album only hit #21 on the charts. But we all still know who they, and lead singer Steve Tyler, are. This rock-and-roll band caught *some* attention right out of the gate, but they built that into a legacy.

I'm looking toward the slow build for my book, snowballing interest and excitement into long-term sales and a devoted readership.

How can you take the long view of book sales?

Spread out your marketing efforts. Rather than focusing all of your efforts upfront, choose strategic activities for your launch and hold off on tasks that can be effectively pursued later down the road. Maybe you need to focus on interviews now and delay the blog tour, or do giveaways at the beginning but hold a larger contest later in the year.

Create a marketing plan calendar. I'm blessed to have a writer friend of mine who sat down and developed a marketing plan for me that goes for a full year. Among her wonderful ideas were capitalizing on special days *throughout the year*—linking my book and sales specials to appropriate holidays or awareness days. Also look for local events, conventions, and ministry conferences that suit your goals.

Engage regularly with your audience. Some authors inundate social media with news, pictures, updates, etc. all around release time, and then it's crickets-and-cicadas for the next six months. Continue to interact with your readers and potential readers! Those who've already read your book will feel more comfortable recommending it to others if you are less spambot and more real person. And potential readers will get that nudge from time to time and may finally buy your book – the one from that nice author they keep seeing.

Write more quality books. Of course, the best long-term approach to selling books is to write more quality books. Having more offerings gives you more shelf space, raises your discoverability in online bookstores, and makes you a brand in readers' minds.

Indeed, I'll be marketing *Hot, Holy, and Humorous* from now until it goes out of print, but I'm also working on the next book. And let's hope that one doesn't release in the same week my other son graduates.

FORTY-EIGHT

Everyday (Budget-Friendly) Marketing Opportunities

Megan DiMaria

When we dream of marketing, we think of big bucks poured into paid advertisements in magazines or online site, eye-catching displays in bookstores, engaging book trailers, or flashy billboards (hey, I told you it was a dream).

Don't lose heart. There are opportunities for everyday marketing that cost little to nothing:

- **Blog**—Maintain a blog.
- **Group blog**—Participating with friends in a themed blog. The upside is that you don't shoulder the entire responsibility to update a group blog. Our WordServe Water Cooler blog has more than 50 contributors.
- **Blog hop/blog tour**—Spread the word about your book by creating a blog tour on friends' and influencers blogs. If you've already published, perhaps some of your readers might be happy to participate.
- **Online radio**—There are several programs interested in hosting authors. Email the hosts to see if there's a good fit. Check out Virtue Radio Network or Blog Talk Radio.
- **eNewsletter**—Whenever you do a book signing or author appearance, provide a sign-up sheet for your

newsletter. Also, make sure readers can sign up on your website, and send readers to sign up from your blog or Facebook. Here are some different options for newsletter programs: Constant Contact, Vertical Response, Your Mailing List Provider, Mail Chimp.

- **Local radio**—Yes, there still are local radio stations that would consider hosting you on one of their programs.
- **City and County TV stations**—I've been fortunate enough to be a guest on two different local TV shows about books and authors. Both of them were affiliated with the community library system. Don't discount this opportunity, both programs were re-run many, many times, and lots of friends and acquaintances mentioned they'd seen the show.
- **Local magazines/weeklies**—send a press release.
- **Library events**—contact your local library to see how they work with authors.
- **Book signing/author events**—My town loves to close down Mainstreet on Sundays from late spring to early autumn for a farmer's market and merchant festival. The library district loans out its booth to local authors. Check with your library PR person or Chamber of Commerce to see if your area has opportunities like this.
- **Twitter**
- **Facebook**
- Be available to **speak** in your community
- Often **employers** will let you mention your new book in their newsletter.

- **Church/community newsletters** might let your place a blurb.
- **College alumni magazine**—Send them a press release about your book.
- I put a notice and some bookmarks on the **community bulletin board** at my neighborhood rec center, and a neighbor I've never met bought four copies and contacted me to sign them for her. Isn't that cool?
- **Charity events**: donate $1 for each book sold at a local event.
- Respond to writers' loop emails, and **be helpful**. Get to know other writers because writers are also readers.
- As soon as you have cover art, **print bookmarks** and pass them out <u>everywhere</u>! I give bookmarks to wait staff at restaurants, people in line at the grocery store, etc. Send them in Christmas cards.
- **Be brave**: discuss your accomplishment everywhere— dentist, pharmacist.
- Put a notice on your website that you will **visit local book clubs** and be available for conference call visits with book clubs.

FORTY-NINE

Marketing Beyond Social Media and the Internet

Melissa K. Norris

We know how powerful social media and the internet can be in marketing and building our author platform. But have you been overlooking your own back yard?

With the launch of my new book, I embarked on traditional online marketing with guest posting, blog tour, and special bonus gifts for those who purchased the book.

But I've had the most sales from my home town. I asked our local pharmacy and grocery store to sell copies of my book. They agreed, and I've sold out at both locations. I made sure to let the owners know I'd be announcing on my social media pages that copies would be available there. (It needs to be a win for both parties.)

We have a local movie theatre that is in the homestretch of fundraising for a new digital projector so they can stay in business. The owner is running an ad for my book in the previews before every movie and selling copies with part of the proceeds going to their digital fund.

I'm teaching two classes for the community. The first was a bread class where I showed how to make artisan bread and thin crust pizza dough. The second is a jelly-making class (all from my book). I sold out of books at the first class with more ordered.

Social media is great, but don't forget about local. Think of places in your home town where people go frequently.

Tips for making businesses say yes to your book:

1. Make an appointment ahead of time with the owner or manager to discuss putting your book in their store. Remember they're busy and show up on time. Think of this like a job interview.

2. Think of ways their business will benefit from having your book.

3. Don't expect them to just let you sell your book without giving it to them at a discount so they make money off the sale too. Be sure you know what your bottom-line price per book is so you both make a profit.

4. Bring a large amount of copies with you, but ask them how many they'd prefer to start with on their store floor.

5. Keep a file at home noting how many books are at each place. Check in on a regular basis to see if they need to be restocked. Make sure they also have your contact info.

FIFTY

Beyond Boring Bookmarks

Michelle Griep

There's no way around it anymore. A writer has to market. You can flail your arms and scream like a little girl all you want, but other than scoring yourself some raised eyebrows or possibly a straitjacket, you *will* need to market your writing. Allow me to teach you the three most important words I taught my children. No, it's not "please" and "thank you" . . . it's "Get over it!"

Now that we're past the lecture, let's move on with some ideas to get your book out there that don't involve the standard lukewarm fare of Twitter and Facebook. Not that I have anything against social media, mind you. It's just that all the authorly Who's from Whoville are already there, shouting their little lungs out.

Create a "Night Out" Event

This is a great way to cross-promote local businesses and your book. Look for small restaurants, clothing stores, kitchen gadget shops, whatever you can possibly tie into your book. Approach them with an idea to have a Women's Night Out or Man Cave Night wherein you'll offer to do a reading, or demonstration, or if you're really confident, to be the chump in a rousing round of Stump the Chump for cheap little prizes.

Meet-Up Groups

Locate some meet-up groups in your area that might be interested in your book. Does your story have a sweet little dog as a character? Find a dog-walking group. In my recent release, *A Heart Deceived*, I talk about the cook's fantastic marmalade, so I'd go for a cooking group. Offer to speak to those groups for free (with a handy-dandy book table at the back for afterwards). Need help finding a group? Meetup is the place for you.

Direct Marketing

Unless you live in Podunksville, USA, you've probably got a local company that ships products directly to customers. Ask if you can place postcards advertising your book in with their shipments. Obviously, if your novel is a romance, you probably don't want a card going out with an order of hedgehog vitamins. Make it related in some way.

Sales Parties

Yes, Tupperware ladies are still around, but they're not the only ones who do in-home parties. Pitch an offer to some reps to come along to one of their shows and do a short reading as an icebreaker. Sales people frequently love opening a conversation with potential buyers by talking about a novel instead of trying to do an immediate hard sell. It gets your name out there, and more importantly, gets people talking about your book.

My latest scheme involves offering a BOGO (Buy One Get One) for my recent release. Since my book is set in England, I used the Keep Calm-o-Matic site to create my own poster. For one weekend, July 12-14, I'm offering to mail a signed copy to anyone who can show me a receipt for a book they've purchased.

Remember: the goal of promoting your work is to entice people to buy. Whapping them upside the head with BUY ME,

BUY ME not only isn't going to work, it's going to annoy potential buyers to swerve way around your train wreck of a marketing ploy.

After all, one can own only so many bookmarks before the recycle bin is filled to the brim.

FIFTY-ONE

Traditional Marketing vs. Relational Marketing

Anita Agers-Brooks

This is how traditional marketing worked:

- Introduce a new or improved product
- Explain all of its cool features
- Show a brief overview highlighting how to use it
- Tell the consumer why they shouldn't live without it
- Communicate a desired call to action

But twenty-first century consumers are more savvy, and demanding. They respond to relational marketing, whereas they are turned off by techniques that proved effective in our not so distant past. Here's the difference:

- Tell a short story about the new or improved product instead of simply introducing it, or even better, show something shocking, dramatic, and/or totally unrelated to get their attention
- Explain how it will benefit the consumer—be clear in communicating what's in it for them
- Paint a picture of a personal connection between the product and the everyday consumer

- Tell the consumer why their life will be better because they have the product, especially if you can make them believe the product will help them fulfill their dreams
- Leave them hanging with just a hint of how they can find out more, or end with a subliminal reminder of the product, but never use in-your-face advertising methods

This is how relational marketing differs.

When marketing our books, we must remember how the consumer has been trained over the last few years. Gone are the days where you could push through advertising. The buying market expects you to ask permission before sending them special offers. Bombarding them with notices about your book or other products mostly ticks them off.

Instead, find a way to connect your message to them personally, and leave the final decision up to them, versus pressuring for a quick decision. Especially effective is making them feel like insiders, and showing them a way they can help. It feeds the human intrinsic motivator to assist others. And psychologically, it establishes a bond—a relationship.

Relational marketing is here to stay. Find a way to establish a relationship with your buying public, create and maintain mutually beneficial reasons to stay connected, and watch your sales rise.

But make your efforts real and genuine. Strive to give them something that truly will make their lives better, because if you try to fake it, your marketing efforts will fall flat. Some things never go out of style. *Honesty. Authenticity. Vulnerability. Humility.* Keep those at your core, and relational marketing will require no more effort than being who you really are.

FAITH HAPPENINGS.COM

Are you a writer or speaker looking to grow your platform, reach and readership?

FaithHappenings.com can help you do just that!

FaithHappenings.com is an online Christian resource with 454 local websites serving more than 31,000 cities and towns. It offers tailored, faith-enriching content for members. Along with a few dozen other benefits, it connects people of faith to information about books, blogs, speaking events, and other resources that interest them most. As a writer or speaker, it will help you connect with people specifically interested in your genre, subject or brand! So, just what can FaithHappenings.com offer you?

On FaithHappenings.com You Can...

1. For Free... **List yourself as a speaker both locally and regionally**—increasing your visibility in multiple markets

2. For Free... **Announce your book signings** in your area

3. **List your books—both traditionally and self-published** (sent out to members who have requested to hear about new books in your genre)*

4. **Announce special e-book promotions the day they happen** (sent out to members and listed on the site daily!)*

5. **Build your blog traffic** by posting your blog into two categories, and be highlighted as a "Featured Blogger" on our Home Page*

6. **Be a highlighted "Author Interview."** FH Daily runs author interviews several times a week. Just email fhdaily@faithhappenings.com to see if you qualify.

7. **Create more awareness for your book with advertising!** An ad on the site is affordable for any author.*

8. As a free member yourself, you can **receive e-mail announcements for any book** in more than 70 genres

What are you waiting for? Get started today by signing up in your local area to become a member at www.faithhappenings.com.
*A small fee applies

FIFTY-TWO

Stealth Marketing

Jan Dunlap

Like many writers, I have issues with shameless self-promotion: I really hate blowing my own horn because isn't that exactly what Christian humility tells us NOT to do? Like every writer, though, I have to get myself into the marketplace to not only make sales and gain a readership, but also to spread the word that God has given me to share.

What's a humble Christian to do?

One answer I've found is what I call 'Stealth Marketing'— marketing that doesn't feel or look like traditional book selling yet still puts my name and book in front of new audiences I might not otherwise reach. Basically, I do non-profit events.

In particular, I donate books to silent auctions or hold a book signing to benefit a local charity. I've found that what I forfeit in cash revenue, I get back many times over in free publicity, good will, new readers, and a personal sense of contribution.

In the past year, I've donated books to local, regional, and national silent auction fundraisers. I started with the annual dinner auction at my children's school, which is usually attended by some 300 people. I wrote up a brief sketch of the book and submitted it along with a photo to be used on the display card at the auction, as well as in the auction booklet. After the event, I had a call from another school parent who told me that she thought the books were such a great item idea that she was going to buy a set of my books to donate to another group's auction. I estimated that would double the exposure I'd just gotten from the first auction. Out of curiosity, I checked my website tracking to find that the number of hits clearly rose after the dinner. Good intentions and a book donation can go a long way, I realized.

Deciding I'd found a productive way to publicize my books and generate sales without the self-promotion I dreaded, I began to look for non-profit groups that corresponded with my target market—birdwatchers and mystery readers—to reach new audiences. In the past year, my books were listed in programs for a variety of fundraisers, including the Raptor Research Foundation's annual (international) meeting, the national conference of MIA/POW families, a Savannah (GA) Rotary Club, and the International Festival of Owls. After each event, I've seen increased traffic to my website.

Closer to home, I really enjoyed the book signing hosted by my favorite local eatery. It was a success for all of us involved: I asked customers to bring items for the local food shelf, and I discounted each book they bought. We collected bags of food to restock the shelves just before the winter holidays, the diner had increased business that morning, and I got free publicity in the bulletins of area churches that support the food shelf, not to mention that warm feeling of doing something good for my community!

FIFTY-THREE

Get a Piece of the Food Craze Pie—It's Not Just for Foodies

Rachel Randolph

Food is everywhere. Take a quick scroll down your Facebook feed. Open up Instagram. Take a peek at your Pinterest boards. Everyone is sharing recipes and pictures of their dinner.

My mom and I have a food blog, where we post recipes and food-related stories (www.welaughwecrywecook.com). That's what we wrote about in our mother/daughter food memoir, so it was obvious for us to blog about food. But did you know you don't have to write about food in your books to get in on the food buzz? Everyone eats, so regardless of what you write about, you have that connection to readers. *Hey, we both eat. What do you know? Maybe we have something else in common.* That's why first dates and client meetings and mixers are almost always food-centered. It's guaranteed common ground. Even if you hate the food, you have something to talk about, right?

If you enjoy cooking, a great way to add new interesting shareable content to your blog is to post an occasional recipe. It's also nice to get all your favorite recipes in one spot online so you can pull them up at the grocery store or on vacation, or easily share them with your family and friends. Next time someone asks you for your pasta salad recipe, the one you bring to every church picnic, you can let them know it's on your blog. You can even hand them your business card with your blog site on it. If you're shy-by-nature like I am, it's an easy, subtle way to share about your books. The card gives them a place to go for the recipe, but also tells them you are an author and speaker. It might just be the events coordinator at your church clamoring for your recipe, and now she has your speaker card and a personal connection to you. See how that works?

Original recipes and pictures make great unique content. But don't worry if your famous pasta salad isn't your own recipe . . . unless, of course, you've been claiming it as your own all these years. If you made a recipe that is not your own, but you really want to share it on your blog, you have a few options:

- Write a post about the recipe, including your own pictures and descriptions of the cooking process, then provide a link to the actual recipe. Food bloggers love this and will often share your post on their networks, and you don't need their permission.

- If you really want to post a full recipe on your site or if it's from a cookbook, you can ask the author for permission. Keep in mind you'll still need to take your own pictures unless the author specifically gives you permission to use hers.

- Make a modified version of the recipe. The Food Blogger Alliance industry standards say this:
    - *If you're modifying someone else's recipe, it should be called '**adapted from**."*
    - *If you change a recipe substantially, you may be able to call it your own. But if it's somewhat similar to a publisher recipe, you should say it's '**inspired***

> *by," which means that you used someone else's recipe for inspiration, but changed it substantially.*

- *If you change three ingredients, you can in most instances call the recipe **yours**.*

As bloggers, it's all about connecting and building a network of like-minded virtual friends. Copyrights on recipes are difficult to claim, but I like to err on the side of attribution. If I took inspiration from a blogger, I at least acknowledge that they had the original idea and I include a link to their version, even if it became something quite different. When adapting a recipe, be sure to write the directions in your own words. They are technically the only part of a recipe that may be covered by copyright laws.

I rarely post a recipe that I merely modified. It just feels wrong to take someone else's creative content. In that case, I might link to the blogger's original recipe and say, "I made So-and-So's recipe for Oatmeal Raisin Cookies and boy, were they delicious. I used almond milk for the dairy milk and used cinnamon instead of nutmeg." I'm still giving my readers value, a yummy adaptable recipe, and networking with another blogger at the same time. Win-win.

Food is meant to be shared. Just keep these guidelines in mind. Then cook, share, repeat.

FIFTY-FOUR

What's YOUR Holiday Plan?

Jan Dunlap

D o you know what today is?

It's National Black Dog Day! Roll out the carpet, crank up the tunes, and open the bags of doggy treats!

In celebration, I'm doing a radio interview, guest posting on several blogs, making a couple of store appearances, and managing a schedule of entertaining tweets, updates, and posts on my own social networks. It's not only a nationally named observance, but it's the perfect opportunity for promoting my very own black dog who stars in my humorous girl-meets-dog memoir, *Saved by Gracie*. Never mind that the book was released last April—today is the day to hit the spotlight again.

In other words, I found a holiday tailor-made for my book, but without all the noise other holidays involve. I don't have to compete with Halloween costumes or décor, Black Friday shopping madness, Santa, New Year's Eve bashes, romantic getaways, or fireworks displays. As a black dog owner, I have the stage all to myself!

How about you? Have you found your tailor-made holiday for book promotion yet?

As every author knows, **timing is one of the best assets you can find in publicity**. Sure, we all wish for something of national importance or interest to pique everyone's interest in our books when they launch, but few of us have any control over those larger scenarios. The key to keeping your book release momentum, then, is to continue to find reasons that your book is timely. Here are a few suggestions for doing just that:

1. **Re-examine your book content for additional audience appeal** you may have missed during the initial book launch. For instance, when my memoir came out, my publisher focused on Christian readers, since it's a tail (I mean *tale*) of spiritual healing. After that first wave of publicity, I began to expand my reach into dog-lover territory by hooking up with animal rescue groups, veterinarians, and dog boutiques. I'm now moving into a third wave of audience strategy by networking with health and wellness groups. Handling all three markets would have been too overwhelming for me to manage at first, but by adding audiences incrementally, I'm better able to market and direct what I need to do next to continue sales.

2. **Pay attention to national news and trends**, and see if you can't jump on those trains. Whenever environmental topics (like wind power vs. natural habitat) are hot, I try to build on those conversations with my own links and commenting, because my **Birder Murder Mystery** series deals with the same topics. The more I engage in the conversations, the better my visibility to my readers, which translates into continued sales, even for older books in my series.

Find your perfect holiday. Does your hero cook Italian food? National Fettuccini Alfredo Day is Feb. 7. Does your book discuss holding onto memories? National Scrapbooking Day is the first Saturday in May. If you write about it, I bet you can find a 'holiday' to connect with it.

FIFTY-FIVE

Market Your Fiction with Nonfiction

Melissa K. Norris

I often hear fiction authors struggling with ways to market their novels. Non-fiction authors seem to have an easier time with marketing, due to their expertise on their subject.

But fiction authors actually have quite a bit of nonfiction in their novels. Remember all that research you've done?

As Christian writers, our characters and story lines have a built-in message of faith. Writing articles on your own faith struggles and how they relate to your character's journey is one way to use nonfiction.

Think about your character's occupation. Is your heroine a landscaper? Write some posts on the best plants in your region. Or tie it in with the setting of your novel. A post on the best plants in the region of your book is even better. You could also spin it and list which plants are best transplanted in any region.

My heroine is a cook on a cattle drive. The pioneers only used cast iron, so I wrote a post on how to care for and use cast iron.

Did you find cool facts when you were researching that didn't make it in to your novel? Then consider writing some articles on these.

These make great blog posts, but try taking it a step further. I pitched the idea to my local newspaper about a monthly column, *Pioneering Today*, which highlights the best of the pioneer lifestyle and how it relates to us today. The editor gave me permission to re-publish the articles on my blog after the current issue has run. I can offer links or pictures, so readers of the newspaper have a reason to visit my website for more information.

Consider magazines or e-zines to submit these articles to as well.

FIFTY-SIX

Promotional Items: The Good and Bad

Jordyn Redwood

I recently returned from the ACFW conference held in Indianapolis. This is an annual gathering of the largest membered group of Christian fiction authors. It's a great time to connect with fellow writers and hope some of the writing genius from authors like Dan Walsh, Tosca Lee, James Scott Bell, and Frank Peretti infuses life into my writing cells.

Most conferences have a "freebie" table where writers are allowed to leave promotional items to get the word out about their product. This year I thought I'd give you my take on them—the good and the bad.

Think of a promotional item with a goal in mind. What do you want it to do for you? Consider the return on your investment and what you hope to achieve. I think most people view a promotional item as a chance for exposure. Most marketing types will tell you it takes six to ten exposures for someone to buy your product. So a good promotional item is something a person will keep and look at over and over.

I've determined that giving away bookmarks is not a good idea. EVERY author/writer does this and last year when I had bookmarks I ended up taking most of them home. They are not unusual enough anymore, and with the advent of e-readers I think many do not *need* them anymore either.

One way bookmarks could work is if you are a very popular, well-known author and they are signed. But, sigh, that is not me. Yet.

My goal was to get people to subscribe to my forthcoming newsletter. I gave out full-size Hershey Bars and packs of gum with stickers on them. The sticker includes a QR code that links to a newsletter sign-up form where I'm giving away a prize worth over $75.00. It includes all three books of my Bloodline trilogy, a $25.00 Amazon gift card, a $25.00 Starbucks gift card and some fun Halloween items and goes on until October 1st.

I brought 108 chocolate bars (okay, I did eat ONE) and 36 packs of gum. I didn't have to bring any home, which was great. People were interested enough to pick them up but, thus far, I've only gotten about six new newsletter subscribers, making it a very expensive venture with few results. Perhaps the QR code is not intuitive for people yet.

Other promotional items and my thoughts.

1. <u>Luggage Tag</u>: This is a good idea because not only do you use it but also other people along the way can see it.

2. <u>Small button flashlights for key chains</u>: I'm iffy on these. The writing on one is hard to read and the light is weak. They are fun to have but I don't know if I would use them.

3. <u>Ribbon bookmark</u>: I'm personally not a fan. I am a no-wrinkle-on-the-pages kind of girl and putting a large plastic paper clip on pages would wrinkle them. Plus, it was not very intuitive to me what it was at first because it was attached to a business card.

4. <u>Pack of sticky notes</u>: This was given out by a publisher. Nice, as most authors love office supplies.

5. <u>A bag of tea</u>: This one I liked because I'm a tea lover. I think this would also be more economical than what I did, as mine ran about 50-60 cents apiece. I think it's a good tie-in for some genres (romance, cozy mystery, historical set in England) but not so much for suspense. It might not work for my books.

6. <u>Small composition notebook</u>: This one I'm actually giving a gold star and I'll tell you why. I still have the one from last year in my purse. Every time I pull it out, I see that author's name. I actually looked into doing this myself but they run (at the cheapest) about $1.00 apiece and that was too spendy for me.

FIFTY-SEVEN

Scenes from a Street Fair

Kimberly Vargas

Writers, have you ever participated in a street fair? I recently had the opportunity to represent local authors through Read Local San Diego at the Encinitas Street Fair. The total cost of the booth for a couple of days was $300.00, broken out into time slots for authors to utilize at the price of $25.00 for a two-hour period. Considering that literally thousands of people attend the annual Encinitas Street Fair (situated two blocks away from the Pacific Ocean), it was clearly a cost-effective way to gain exposure in the community.

Parking nearby was out of the question. My husband was good enough to drop me off near the booth, using back roads to weave in and out. Realizing this would be the case, I took a roller bag with wheels to carry my books, a desk easel to display my books at the booth, several pens, a pad of paper, and a set of business cards. As far as the number of books, they suggested at least five, so I brought twenty. Next time, I'll go with around forty or fifty. I pre-signed the books with a "hope you enjoy the read" type message, so I could quickly fill in people's names and the dates and facilitate the process.

There were three other authors at the booth with me. We had two six-foot tables, with two authors per a table. "Oh, you're here," my table mate said when I arrived about five minutes before our shift began. "I was about to take over your table space."

I became acquainted with him and the other three authors in my shift. At first, none of us were sure of how to engage the throes of people walking by our booth. One author called to people like a carnival barker, offering a chance to win one of his books if people would fill out a slip with their email and mailing addresses. Most folks, there with the intention of being out for a stroll and buying no greater purchase than a funnel cake, weren't too receptive to this approach. The four of us did some brainstorming, and giveaways seemed to be the way to go in this environment. I gave away free signed copies, asking for an honest review on Amazon in lieu of payment. That seemed to go over pretty well. In each book, I placed a business card with my contact information on one side and my book cover on the other side.

Next to our booth was a fifth local author, a gentlemen of a certain age who writes for the Young Adult market. He has quite a following and teenagers kept coming by throughout the day to say hello to him. He has nineteen books to his credit and required his own booth. He is an adjunct professor at a local university and asked if I would like an opportunity to speak and / or teach. The street fair was proving to be a good opportunity to interact not just with the public, but with like-minded authors.

During the slow moments of the shift, our group compared notes and talked shop. An elderly man in the group who was intimidated by social media went home with an education about how to use Twitter. One lady needed a reasonably priced editor and received a referral. Another writer needed a graphic artist referral for book covers, and was given several suggestions. I became familiar with the San Diego Writers Guild and started looking into their upcoming meetings.

We also worked as a team, which was fun. If someone approached an author whose book wasn't their cup of tea, then there were four other writers of very different genres available to meet. Several authors had huge display posters with the covers of their books. They said these can be ordered online, and all one has to do is send in the content and a digital file. We learned that coffee and books and wind are not a very smart combination. We learned that a roll of duct tape is imperative in order to fix issues such as crooked signs or tent tables that needed more infrastructure. Bringing a box of pens and having a way to make change is also advised.

All in all, a street fair is probably not going to yield thousands of sales, unless the fair specifically focuses on books. Most people going to a street fair may not have books on the mind, but it is a wonderful networking opportunity, and you just can't beat the exposure for the price. You may want to check out street fairs and rental booths in your own area, because people really do like to support local businesses, including their local writers and authors.

FIFTY-EIGHT

Direct Mail—Cool as Ever

Kimberly Vargas

Have you ever sent a letter to prospective customers asking them to buy one of your books? If so, you have participated in direct mail marketing—one of the most efficient and effective selling techniques. If you think it's too old school for you, then consider this: 55 percent of Americans read the news, 95percent have telephones, 98 percent have television sets. However, 100 percent of Americans have a mailbox. Therefore, it is your only 100 percent opportunity to hone in on your targeted audience.

There are four components to a successful direct mail campaign: the **Creative**, the **List**, the **Offer** and the **Results**.

1) **Creative**: Of course you want your direct mail piece to be eye-catching and informative. How you present your offer to your list has to be done professionally so that all of the emotional hot buttons are triggered while also maintaining interest and going for the sale. Some of the best copywriters are paid thousands of dollars to write a single sales pitch letter, simply because the creative aspect of your campaign is that important. If your budget allows it, consider using variable data printing, which personalizes each letter to its recipient using demographics such as male/female, geographic region, etc. Even just a first name is effective in grabbing attention.

2) **List**: Although your current customer base is incredibly valuable, it will be necessary to continuously seek out new customers as well. Your current customers will only buy so much. Aside from that, you will lose customers every year for various reasons. A good way to replace your eroding customers is by acquiring targeted mailing lists. It's great to have a fantastic book but unless you can get it in front of the correct audience, it's all for naught. The best list for you may be expensive, and you can expect to pay per name. The more targeted the list of prospects, the better. If you are selling a book on, say, surfing, you want to find a list of people who surf AND who buy books on surfing. If you get a list that is cheap or free, that doesn't mean it's a good one. In fact, you want to be absolutely sure you have a solid list before you start sending out direct mail offers and accruing postage fees. Acxiom® and Dun & Bradstreet® are examples of companies that sell lists. You can also work with a direct mail advertising company who can walk you through the entire campaign, such as Modern Postcard.

3) **Offer**: What you offer in the direct mail campaign needs to be exclusive to the group, while also being priced to make a profit for you. Make an offer that will get the recipient to act quickly, such as directing them to your website to see a sample chapter, free gift or autographed copy if they respond by a certain date. The options are unlimited, so you can test lots of different ideas to see which offers produce the best outcomes.

- Keep the offer simple: One or two *QUICK* benefits: "Save time and money with our services!" or "Stay warm this winter!"
- Give a reason to continue reading: "See the other side for big savings!"

- Make a big promise and be sure you can fulfill it: "Order now and enjoy a full head of hair in three weeks!"
- Include an expiration date . . . create a sense of urgency or exclusivity. The most compelling direct mail pieces have a call to action.

4) **Results**: A direct mail campaign which produces more than a 2% response is considered successful. Lower than a 1% response is typical. You then need to take into account the conversion rate (the conversion of responses into sales), assuming the campaign is designed to produce responses or inquiries and not just actual sales.

Do not engage in a 100,000-piece nationwide mailing your first time out of the gate. Try 500 or so at first and see how it goes. This way you can tweak the results, eliminate certain demographics, and introduce others. Think of this kind of marketing as a long play that takes some honing. Aside from sales, some additional metrics to consider are the number of orders, how many offers were redeemed, how many responses by phone / email you received, and the estimated future value of your new customers. Track your responses carefully. Enter them into a CRM system like ACT!®, Goldmine®, Salesforce®, etc., put them into an Excel spreadsheet, put them in a box or record them in a notebook. Track them and make sure they are updated regularly, if possible. A mail house can assist you by checking your list against their national change of address software, and provide you with any move updates so you can follow your customer base.

Not all books can be sold successfully through direct mail. The topic must be of interest to the targeted audience and the price must be sufficiently low to encourage people to respond with an order. Tell them why the information in your book will be of interest to them.

In closing, you might find it interesting to know that direct mail came back in a big way in 2011, increasing by $10 billion and gaining another 5% in terms of total ad spend share. Each dollar spent on direct marketing yields, on average, a return on investment of $12.05. By comparison, each dollar spent on non-direct mail advertising yields an ROI of $5.29. (Source: DMA's *Power of Direct Marketing; 2011 Edition*).

FIFTY-NINE

20 Reasons Books Don't Sell

Greg Johnson

When your book doesn't move off the shelves or Amazon warehouses in vast quantities, our first tendency is to point fingers. There is something deep in the human psyche that needs to blame someone when hopes, dreams and plans don't work out. Publishers blame authors, authors blame publishers (or their agents), retail might blame marketing.

The truth is, there will never be one reason why a particular book doesn't sell. All any of us—author, publisher, agent, retail partner—can do is look in the mirror and ask, "Did I personally do all I could to help the process?" The other truth is, everyone who invests time in writing, agenting, editing, packaging, marketing, publishing, and selling a book wants the book to turn a profit. We *all* want books to sell . . . every single book! Otherwise, none of us could stay in business. So let's disabuse ourselves of mistrusting motives of the key people trying to help our book—everyone wants to stay in business!

So why don't books sell? It's usually not because of a lack of desire, or effort, or skill, or hope, or prayer . . . it's a myriad of tangible and intangible factors. Some an author can control, some a publisher can, and many are outside the control of anyone.

Welcome to the world of publishing in the 2010s. Times . . . they have changed. So what are the reasons a good book may not have great sales?

1. Hundreds of books have been scuttled because a war or national tragedy took center stage right when a book releases. Suddenly, all of the great PR efforts and TV interviews set up get pre-empted, never to be rescheduled because everyone has moved onto the newest front list of books to promote.

2. A bad package. It doesn't happen too often these days; publishers like to make authors/agents happy. But cover designs do sell—or not sell—books. A great title that screams "must read," a subtitle that grabs, back cover copy that says, "keep looking," engaging table of contents, endorsements or a foreword by someone of note, a compelling first few pages . . . these are a few factors that can turn a book browser into a buyer.

3. Champions leave. With uncertainty in the industry and publisher entrenchment these last five years, editors have been leaving or moving to different jobs at an enormous clip. Without an in-house champion to keep the book on track, details often fall through the cracks no matter who is following up. New editors must inherit projects, but if they didn't acquire them, sometimes those books get treated like the red-headed step-child.

4. Marketing/PR failures. A publisher had no effective marketing plan, or didn't work their marketing plan no matter the agent effort or follow up. The truth is, the 80/20 principle is truer in publishing than likely anywhere else. Eighty percent of publishers' marketing

money goes to 20 percent of their books, because 80 percent of their income comes from 20 percent of their books. A huge fact of life in a very tough publishing environment. Sadly, these days, it may even be 90/10.

5. <u>Author ambivalence.</u> An author decided they'd let others do the heavy lifting in creating awareness about the book. The writer took the attitude that "Everyone, other than me, should tell the world about my book—because I don't want to be seen as commercializing anything; I'm above that." Or, "God has called me to write, not to market my writing." Or, "I'm busy writing my next book. I don't have time." Or, "I'm just not good at pushing my own stuff." Spiritualizing or tossing out excuses about your inactivity likely means one thing in today's book culture: a short writing career. God will more often "bless" hard and smart work. If you don't believe in your work enough to champion it, rethink book publishing. Or, perhaps become a collaborator; you can write and not have to worry about promotion.

6. <u>Author platform.</u> Ah yes, the scourge of authors everywhere. If you haven't built enough potential readers into your sphere of influence through blogging, speaking, radio or social networking, publishers will just often say, "We can't help you." Why? See reason 20.

7. <u>Friendship failure.</u> An author's famous friends (the ones your proposal said were on board) who promised to blog, tweet and Facebook about it forgot, or got too busy, or finally read your book and didn't like it, or have been doing too much of it for every other author friend

they have and are just tired of filling their social net-working space crowing about someone else's product (when they have their own to PR).

8. <u>Small target audience.</u> The book doesn't meet a broad enough felt need. Niche books used to have a chance. These days they often do not.

9. <u>Topic overpopulated.</u> The book has been done a million ways from Sunday and there is just too much competition on the subject.

10. <u>The book is poorly written.</u> You didn't get a good edit. This is more common with independently-published authors who don't pay for developmental or copy edits, but not unheard of in traditional publishing.

11. <u>All we hear is crickets.</u> The book never got word of mouth or enough great reviews (50+). There is no tangible buzz about you as an author or the book. Like a movie that no one talks about will sink after week two, the same is nearly true with books. Most books can sell 3,000 to 5,000 copies with little buzz. But if a book has sold more than 10,000 copies, it's because people are talking.

12. <u>Publisher oversight.</u> The e-book didn't release simulta-neously—and in effect the marketing and PR upon the book's initial release went to naught—without the e-product available "on the shelves" during the launch. Years ago, one marketing director I was dealing with didn't know Facebook could be used to promote a book (luckily his PR person did). While gross incompetence is rare, mistakes happen out of the control of the author or agent.

13. <u>A book was written and it should have been an article.</u>
    We've all read books that were all but over after chapter
    4. The story was predictable or the points over-used.
    Yes, there is nothing new under the sun, but try to make
    sure you're conveying content that you can't get in a few
    blogs.

14. <u>One careless word.</u> The book had a swear word in it so
    Lifeway wouldn't carry it. This happens a fair amount
    of times because authors insist that profanity makes it
    more "real" (which it might) and they'd rather sacrifice
    sales than not be real. As Dr. Phil would say, "How's that
    working out for you?" If you want to play in certain
    sandboxes, you have to play by the sandbox's rules.
    Sorry.

15. <u>Setting and storyline.</u> If it's fiction, having a setting out-
    side of America, England or Ireland. "Because I love
    Russia (or Africa or Thailand)" just plain rarely sells
    well in America. Or having a storyline that is not enter-
    taining—and very hard—to read (i.e. child abuse, sexual
    abuse, deaths of key characters).

16. <u>Changing reading habits.</u> People don't read as much as
    they used to. Or if they do, it's blogs and articles that are
    free on the web. More true with nonfiction readers.
    The attention span of today's internet-soaked reader
    has shortened radically.

17. <u>Cheap buyers.</u> People are waiting around for the free or
    cheap e-book that comes out a year later instead of
    spending $10 to $20 on a new book they know they will
    get eventually and pay less (or nothing) for. Also, the
    proliferation of self-pub'd books that have a lower price
    tag has put a dent in a traditional author's sales.

18. <u>Life happened.</u> Something happened in the author's life so that all of their well-laid plans to launch and promote their book flew out the window. Or it happened to the in-house PR person's life. Or the outside PR person's life. Or the agent's life. Or their famous author friends' lives. "Life happens" all the time, and I've seen more than a few books sink because cancer or a death occurred in the family of some key person trying to make the book a success.

19. <u>Book retail has gone bye-bye.</u> If you're a Christian writer, the lack of stores to sell into can certainly be one place to put the blame. When I first started as an agent 21 years ago, there were 6,500 Christian bookstores. Now there are about 1,000. So . . . "no one walks into Christian bookstores anymore" is fairly true.

20. <u>The industry.</u> Frankly, publishing is hard. Every publishing house is working harder for less money. Every editor, marketing and PR person, sales person . . . is overloaded with work because margins are thin. If there is a "new normal" that will get us back to center in publishing, it hasn't happened yet.

These 20 reasons, and likely a few others, would all not count a bit if people could just find out about the new books they want to read. Agents and editors are still finding great stories, fabulous writers and motivated publishers. The problem? Creating awareness for these great books! Retail continues to shrink, magazines are all but gone, and with over 100,000 *new* bloggers (on WordPress alone) starting blogs *every day*, it's only a matter of time before most of us are tuning out all of the content coming into our inbox (if we haven't already). How will people start finding out about all of these good books?

The newest and biggest elephant in the publishing room is this: **How, with the demise of print media and bookstores, do we find and target regular book-buying readers who are interested in a particular genre and book topic?**

Faithhappenings.com was created to help answer this question. FaithHappenings offers the following unique benefits to authors, publishers and reader-consumers:

- When a member checks specific boxes on their preferences, it will send readers an email when a new book comes out in any genre they enjoy and buy.
- FaithHappenings also lists music and videos, independently published books and music, local events of every type, scripture, blogs, devotionals and much more . . . and all a member has to do is check a box to find out about them. It only takes three minutes to fill out a profile, and it is free to do so.

Check out www.faithhappenings.com. There are 454 local websites that carry local and national info, with a big emphasis on books!

VI.

Get Out There:
Promotional Events

SIXTY

Antisocial Media

Kimberly Vargas

G od bless the internet.

It's the great equalizer of our time. It has been a tour de force for introverts the world over who feel more confident and less prone to risk behind a laptop than a podium. Marketing no longer is the exclusive playground of handsome and highly articulate extroverts, people that really know how to connect with other people. A website can have an infinite amount of charm—or at least charm enough not to require a spokesmodel.

How has this been possible? One reason is a fundamental shift in marketing itself and how society sees it. Marketing strategy has evolved from outbound to inbound. An outbound marketing strategy involves actively finding people and making them aware of your product and offerings. An inbound marketing strategy is about being easy to find. It requires a high level of visibility. If you are invisible to Google, it's not going to work.

This being said, I recently met with a visibility coach to discuss the next steps for how to continue building a writing platform. It seemed like many bases had been covered, and now I was stuck on how to proceed. After all, the infrastructure seemed to be coming along:

- Website
- Blog
- Writing contest award site

- Book reviews
- Smashwords and Amazon purchase links
- Facebook
- LinkedIn
- Pinterest board
- YouTube radio interview
- Google Adwords, Google+

I reviewed all of these facets of the marketing platform with the visibility coach. She was glad that some visibility had already been created, but there was still a lot to do. She said that the aforementioned social media sites are tools. Such tools are only part of a marketing strategy's infrastructure and did not constitute its entirety.

Some of the things I had been putting off on my to-do list started coming back to mind:

- Determine how many prospective customers would be interested in your product
- Define that group—Who are they? How old are they? What is their demographic data?
- Create a buzz among that target profile
- Identify their buying behavior
- Develop a message that speaks to that group
- Become highly visible to that customer group
- Learn their communication style and preferred methods of contact

The coach said, "I think we need to get you some REAL fans and not just virtual ones." She kind of laughed a little bit, and I hadn't realized until then that it was kind of funny. All my supporters are either friends or ones I've garnered online. "Virtual fans are all well and good, but you need to meet and connect with some REAL people, some actual people now. We're going to move forward with a press release and creating some *events*."

The coach could probably tell that I was a little uneasy about the whole '*events*' thing. It's awkward enough pumping up a site with one's name and picture on it in cyberspace. How could I look people in the eye and do it for real? I would know if they didn't really want to meet me. What if someone told me to get lost? What if they said they had already read my book and they thought I was destroying literature or something? Besides, I had never met any of the authors I had always admired. Was that really necessary? Talking about my work with strangers . . . ugh. It seemed like the worst kind of vanity.

But the visibility coach pointed out something enlightening. When positioning the book and other works to the audience, there is no reason to focus on the author. The focus is on the characters in the book. She said to become the cheerleader of my main characters and pump them up constantly—and to take myself out of the equation. That resonated with my introverted nature, and I breathed a little easier.

Marketing is about telling a story. Who better to market, then, than us storytellers?

The ancient concept of the group storyteller conjures up images of tribes fixated on a speaker, basking in the orange glow of a campfire. That kind of storytelling is interactive. Actors are storytellers, but of a different sort. They tell stories with their physical beings—not with words.

Writing, as a form of storytelling, can't be purely antisocial because life and the human experience aren't antisocial. That's the whole point. People are trying to connect and feel something. The internet has made it very easy to forget that—but people go to the movies and read books for a reason. They are looking to connect. And as uncomfortable as it may be at times, connections just do not belong in the realm of the antisocial.

SIXTY-ONE

Your Basic Marketing Tool Kit

Jan Dunlap

Your book is published! Congratulations! Now you have to go out and sell it, which generally means you'll be doing book signings, giving talks, and attending festivals. Before you walk into your first event, assemble a marketing tool bag you can use at every venue you visit. Even when you're being hosted by a book store who will be handling all the purchases, you still need some basic promotional tools to make the most of the marketing opportunity. Here's what goes in a basic author marketing bag:

1. **Bookstand.** You want to be able to prop up a copy of your book so everyone can see the cover. A simple acrylic one works just fine, and you can find it at office supply stores. In fact, pick up two!

2. **Signage.** You want to provide important information for your buyers: price, perhaps a short glowing review, method of payment. Again, acrylic sign holders are at the local office supply store, and they come in a variety of sizes. I use one 8x11 size to display buying information, and I have a 4x6 sign set up next to a small tub inviting folks to sign up for my newsletter. Depending on the event, you can easily customize the sign each time by printing a new one from your home computer. For example, when I'm donating part of my proceeds to

a special charity or offering a multiple book price, I can include that on the sign.

3. **Newsletter sign-up sheet/collection box.** I have a small plastic container with pens and little notepads in it for people to use to leave their email address for my newsletter subscriber list. I also have a small book-related prize sitting next to the box; every month I draw a winner from those addresses and send out the prize.

4. **Tablecloth.** Your host may not have a tablecloth for your use, and you'll wish you had one. It gives you that professional look!

5. **Handout.** Depending on your budget and creativity, this can be anything that will remind the customer about you once you're no longer in sight. Bookmarks and postcards printed with your book cover work nicely. Do you write sweet romances? Give out candy kisses!

6. **Credit card reader.** I resisted getting one for my first few years as an author, and it was a mistake. Few people have the cash on hand to buy your book if you're doing direct selling, and the last thing you want is for someone who wants to buy the book right then and there to have to walk away and buy it later. . . because chances are very good that it won't happen. Research the different options available. I use Phoneswipe, and I know many authors who use Square.

7. **Cash.** Some folks do use currency, so you'll want to bring some cash to make change. I keep a **small zipper case** in my marketing bag with enough change for five books, and it doubles as a place to keep any cash payments secure.

SIXTY-TWO

Four Lessons from the Speaking Circuit

Bob Welch

For 20 years now I've dragged a suitcase of books from speaking event to speaking event, telling stories, signing books, listening to people in line innocently yammering on while someone else is waiting impatiently to get an autograph.

I've spoken from the Statehouse in Boston to a rain-tattered canopy outside a fire hall while firefighters let children blast the siren, from hotel ballrooms with nearly 500 people to three people in an assisted-living home, two of whom seemed comatose by the time I'd finished my intro.

Here, then, are four bits of advice about using your speaking engagements to sell books, 19 of which I've written, a few of which have actually sold:

Go where you're wanted.

I've spent far too much of my life trying to convince people that they should believe in me and far too little time appreciating those who do. In the last few years, though, I've wised up.

Push on the doors, sure. Push hard. But if they don't open, stop pushing and go find another door that might. Don't let your pride get in the way. It's far more fun doing a small-time gig where people appreciate your being there than beating your head on the door of some larger or more prestigious organization or event that never will.

Partner with one person who believes in you in the community where you're going to speak.

It was a blustery, rainy Friday night, and I had a speaking gig "up river" in a small community. I honestly wondered if anyone other than the woman who'd organized the talk would come.

After the event, I walked out to my car with more than $500 in book sales, a stomach full of homemade pie and an evening of memories with a bunch of warm, wonderful people.

Why? Because that one woman was an "influencer," someone people along the river respected. An organizer, someone who can bring an event together. An ally, someone who believed in me.

Someone like that can do more to help your event be a success than hundreds of tweets.

Take time to get to know the place where you're speaking or the organization you're speaking to.

Whether you're selling books afterward or not, this is simply the right thing to do. Why do concert crowds go nuts when some well-known performer mentions something about their town? Because people take pride in where they live and appreciate it when others do, too.

It shows respect. It shows you care. It shows that you're not just "mailing it in."

In one of my books, *52 Little Lessons from It's a Wonderful Life,* I devote a chapter to a simple remark that one of the heavenly angels says to Clarence Odbody before the "Angel Second Class" is sent to earth to help a desperate George Bailey: "If you're going to help a man, you want to know something about him, don't you?"

Take the time to know something about your audience. Don't just do a couple of Google searches. Talk to your host. Make a few calls. Do some reporting.

Finally, be interesting.

Never have people had so many options with which to spend their time, so many excuses for not leaving their home.

So, if they're giving up an evening for you, forget the "first, do no harm" edict inaccurately linked to the Hippocratic Oath. (By me in one book!) No, first, do not put people to sleep. Say something that people haven't heard before. Or say it in a way they haven't heard before. Tell jokes. Dispense information. Inspire life-changing action.

But, above all, be interesting. I recently went to an author's event just to see what other writers do. The guy spent the entire evening reading from his book.

Yawn.

That's the reader's job. As writers, we should spend our time offering audiences insight that our books do not. Our stories might be the impetus that draws people to our events, but give them something more than a rehash of our book or books. Besides, if you're interesting, people are more apt to believe your books will be, too. And there's no better way to be asked back.

SIXTY-THREE

How to Plan a Successful Book Signing

Julie Cantrell

As a first-time author of two children's books, *God is with Me through the Day* and *God is with Me through the Night*, I was surprised to discover that the most challenging part of the journey was marketing.

I had worked as a marketing writer for years; but marketing my own work was . . . well . . . icky. As a friend put it: "It's a bit like standing in front of the mirror with a stranger and asking them to say nice things about you."

Despite my reluctance, I was grateful to experience many successful book signings after the launch of my children's books. When I sold more than 100 books at several signings, the bookstore managers were amazed. They couldn't believe I was having such strong turnouts as a first-time author.

One Barnes & Noble community resource manager hit the nail on the head when he said he'd never had an author market the event as much as I had. That behind-the-scenes work was responsible for the second-largest signing of his career.

When planning your next author event, keep these tips in mind:

1. **Your biggest ally is word of mouth.** Reach out to anyone you know in a community and ask them to invite friends,

family, neighbors, church members, school peers, etc. You'd be surprised how interested folks become when they have a personal connection to the author.

2. **Send out press releases to local media outlets**. Look for television news programs and radio shows that routinely support local events. Contact regional magazines, and reach out to the newspapers for a book review and/or author interview.

3. **Post the event on all community calendars,** since many media outlets will share the event both online and in print.

4. **Contact local churches** to invite their church community to join you. You can also offer to visit the church for a personal author event. Some churches have been extremely kind and generous to me by promoting the event in their Sunday Bulletin or weekly newsletter.

5. **Use the internet to locate your target audience** and reach out to them via email, direct mail, phone calls, or—of course—word of mouth. Depending on your book, you may want to contact veterans groups, healthcare workers, mothers groups, or schools.

6. **Use key social networking tools** such as Facebook, Twitter, and a personal blog to boost interest in your books. Also consider pitching high-traffic blogsites to serve as a guest blogger.

7. **Don't be shy.** When you're at the event, engage attendees in conversation. Remember, humor is key. Get people laughing and they'll want to hear more. Marketing does take time, but the extra hours pay off in most cases.

SIXTY-FOUR

Small Pond, Big Splash

Dianne Christner

Make a Splash!
On my recent mini book tour, I discovered how easy it is to create major buzz in a small geographical pocket. Since Phoenix has 1.5 million residents, I haven't made much of a local splash for all my marketing efforts. Call me a city girl, but you can imagine how thrilled I was to create major splash in several small communities?

I chose a small Ohio town (the setting of my novel) and an Indiana Mennonite community because my characters are, yes, Mennonite. In twelve short days, I connected with hundreds of people who started a local buzz about my books. I did my part, and the rest just happened.

Imagine hundreds of rocks simultaneously tossed into water. The ripples intersect and make a major splash. The same disturbance would go unnoticed in the ocean, but is visible in a pond.

Helpful Tips for a Mini Book Tour

Establish a relationship with local influencers. They work hard on your behalf. Influencers booked my speaking engagement, organized book signings, and blogged and promoted my events. They placed newspaper notifications *for me*. See what I mean about easy?

Keep costs down. If you need to buy books, don't over purchase (like I did) unless you wish to haul them around. I left unsold books with influencers. I did cover half of my expenses, and I'm sure I can do better next time.

Book at least one paid speaking event. My event had 200-plus guests. I sold 40 books and gave free handouts with my contact information. It was a bonus when a newspaper reporter covered the event.

Take a guestbook to your events. I didn't, but I will next time! A guestbook would provide a relaxing way to get name spellings, information, and jot notes for later—all while making pleasant conversation with readers. I frantically jotted notes that got shoved into my purse. Not very professional.

Attend local events, even if it's not your event. When a book tour is the reason for your visit to a community, the topic naturally accompanies personal introductions.

Giveaways. Offering *free* bookmarks opens conversations with people who wouldn't otherwise make eye contact. Book giveaways are both promo and ministry. Trust God with your offerings.

Get prayer support. I would have remained fearful and frazzled without my prayer support team. Thanks guys!

Take your vitamins. Even good stress is hard on the immune system, and I ended up going to Urgent Care two days upon my return. (Probably because I was an introvert on overload)

Benefits and Blessings
- Meeting local authors

- Opportunity to sign shelved books in local bookstores and gift shops.
- Networking — (Got featured in summer reading group. *They approached me!*)
- Media/newspaper coverage
- Unexpected opportunities —Books placed in church and school libraries
- Purchasing items for future promo. Of course I bought a handcrafted Amish doll.
- Photographing opportunities for website, blog, and promo use
- Research for blogging topics
- Gleaning new information about the book industry
- Ministry — planting spiritual seeds and encouraging readers
- Personal growth

SIXTY-FIVE

With Us Here Tonight

Jan Dunlap

Shortly after my first book was published, I gave a book talk at our local library.

Then I gave another talk at another library. And then a third library.

Then a Rotary Club called me. A few months later, I found myself the featured speaker at a Shriners dinner. Last month I presented a talk at the National Eagle Center. Birding festivals, book conferences, annual meetings, schools, service organizations--I've addressed them all.

Wait a minute. I thought I was a writer, not a speaker.

Guess what? Book authors get to do both!

The fact is, you NEED to do both if you're going to successfully build your readership and market your writing. That means you should work on your public speaking skills, and the best way to do that is to take every opportunity you find for a speaking engagement. Develop the following five types of speeches, and you'll be ready for anyone!

The **Sound Bite** is the one you will use a bazillion times. It's the one-liner you'll utter every time someone asks you what your book is about. It's also one of the hardest to compose because you need to distill your book and its value down to one sentence. My sound bite for my series is: "The Birder Murders is a humorous series about a really nice guy who happens to find bodies when he's out birding."

The **Book Talk** is the speech that focuses on your book's content. If it's nonfiction, you can give a general review of the topic itself, or focus on just one chapter's point and why it's important. If it's fiction, you discuss characters, their relationships, the plot, how you came up with all of it, what you want to accomplish with it. This works best with audiences who have already read your book because they will have questions about what they've learned and/or enjoyed from reading it.

The **Business Talk** is about your experience with the publishing business of being an author. The changes we've seen in publishing, including the growth of e-books and marketing paradigms, is a topic that appeals to audiences composed of business people or future authors.

The **Writing Talk** is about your own process of writing a book. Do you do research? Conduct interviews? Journal or set word goals? The beauty of a Writing Talk is that it is appropriate for a variety of groups, and depending on the slant you give it for the group you're addressing, it works equally well as a classroom talk, a keynote address for a gathering of library supporters, an awards speech, a writers conference, a book club . . . you name it.

The **Topic Talk** is the newest talk in my own arsenal of speeches. Because my books are about nature, I've started giving talks about nature education and conservation issues. If it is mentioned in my books, it's fair game for a talk and a great way to use extra research.

Visit www.toastmasters.com for more great resources to help you to continue to develop your public speaking skills.

SIXTY-SIX

Marketing In and Out of the Box for Authors and Speakers

Anita Agers-Brooks

I*t's getting harder to find places to sell books."*
Public speaking is still the most effective sales tool for book authors according to many professionals. But with conference attendances lowering, and some closing down, the opportunities are dwindling.

And without a strong marketing plan, you often can't get a publisher to bite on a proposal anyway.

So what's an author to do?

You've probably heard "think outside the box" when it comes to marketing, but what does that mean?

Don't lose hope—there are still effective things you can do to strengthen your marketing strategy through speaking. For instance, re-slant your messages to fit groups you might not normally speak to, or have never thought of speaking to.

- If you speak on marriage, have you targeted business groups and associations where couples may work together, or have employees who do?
- If parenting is your theme, have you contacted day-care centers who often spend more waking hours with children than parents?

- If grief or trauma is your message, what about speaking to Chambers of Commerce, or association conferences about how their members can help the hurting, promote good will, and further their mission as a result?
- Is there an awards banquet you can connect a presentation to?

When contacting churches and ministry organizations, ask yourself questions like these:

- What are the biggest problems I see in society today?
- What are my greatest pet peeves?
- What do I hear people complain about most often?
- What do people say they are lacking?

Those are the areas you can target to reach audiences in a relevant way. Many ministries are looking for speakers who can address concerns of a younger crowd growing more jaded, more "accepting," and more in need of spiritual wisdom than ever—but who can deliver that message wrapped in practical twenty-first century applications.

The fact is, human beings all over the planet are drawn to messages of hope and encouragement, and like-minded people flock together. The key is to develop a strategic marketing plan, do your homework, study potential audiences, make consistent contacts, and follow up on a regular basis. Over time you will begin to get a feel for what works and what doesn't. Set goals and stick to them.

Finally, I must mention the most important thing of all: partnering with God through prayer, trust, AND practical action.

Here's my real secret to any marketing success. Based on the Parable of the Talents in Matthew 25, I ask God who the bankers are that He wants me to invest my talents with, and then I look and listen. I'm often surprised at the opportunities available; it simply takes looking at things through fresh eyes. Sometimes in the box, and sometimes by stepping out.

SIXTY-SEVEN

Overcoming Your Speaking Fears to Market Your Books

Anita Agers-Brooks

Does terror of speaking in front of crowds threaten to paralyze your writing career?

Imagine a large stadium filled to capacity. The announcer introduces the main speaker. The audience claps and cheers. Adrenaline pulses in a flood through your veins. You approach the podium in slow-motion, while your legs beg to run away as fast as they can.

You arrive at the center of the stage, open the presentation slides on your electronic tablet, even as you pray you don't make a fool of yourself. Your mouth opens, at the same time the heel of your hand brushes the edge of the tablet, knocking it on the ground. The clatter echoes across the hushed platform. Your fingers tremble as you lift the darkened screen. You scan the crowd in front of you; noticeable fidgeting causes a contagious rustle. You clear your throat, offer a half-smile, and scramble to remember what your notes said.

Once again, your lips part, but instead of a greeting, a guttural growl boomerangs through the microphone.

Is this a nightmare for anyone but me?

These days, whether writing non-fiction or novels, authors need to work twice as hard as public speakers to market their books.

But why do our minds threaten to sabotage us when we stand in front of smiling faces, in a sea of expectant people clamoring to hear the messages we've waited to share? Are we doomed to fail when panic replaces our passion? What goes on inside our brains?

Though I agree with most people who rank public speaking in their top five worst fears, there are tips I've learned to help reduce my anxiety.

1. *Study your material intently.*

2. *Practice in front of a mirror.*

3. *Read the Bible.* This simple answer saved me in the past, when anxiety medication, panic inhibiting techniques, and other methods failed to help me move past fear. I discovered that immersing myself in God's Word calmed my frazzled nerves.

4. *Follow sound advice.* The Anxiety Coach (www.anxietycoach.com) offers practical instructions to settle emotions that threaten to keep you from spreading your message.

5. *Wear comfortable clothing.* Function along with your fashion.

6. *Get serious about laughter.* Humor relaxes emotions, body, mind, and spirit. Watch a funny program immediately before leaving to speak. Read a riotous book or article. Listen to a comedic CD or download on your way to the presentation.

7. *Thirty minutes before speaking, drink water* to hydrate your vocal chords, brain cells, and emotional sensors. Water is a miracle drug. (Thirty minutes should allow your body time to shed waste, so you can visit a restroom before taking the stage.)

8. *Prior to walking onto your platform, breathe in slowly through your nose,* count to ten, and release slowly through your mouth. Repeat twice, so you follow the process a minimum of three times.

9. *Prayer walk to the front of your audience.*

10. *Don't make a big deal out of flubs.* Remember, most audiences won't recognize mistakes, so carry on, or make light of it. Besides, mess-ups make us more human to observers.

Speaking is part of the modern writing model, but no need to worry. You can overcome and share with confidence.

SIXTY-EIGHT

Creative Venue Planning

Jan Dunlap

If bookstores are the only place you're signing and talking about your books, then you're missing the boat.

Perhaps even literally.

In the last year, in addition to bookstores, I've talked and signed books at gift shops, diners, book club gatherings, Rotary Club breakfasts, libraries, senior community dinners, and summer festival booths. Since my novels are about a bird lover, I've also signed books at bird feeding supply stores and an annual birding meeting, not to mention an international owl festival, a regional hummingbird celebration, and the National Eagle Center. At every venue, I've sold more books than I have at any bookstore signing, not to mention the new readers I've found and the publicity such events generated.

So how do you pack your calendar with venues that will work hard for you? The answer is Creative Venue Planning, and here's my three-step recipe:

1. Look past your story, and instead, **brainstorm your book's topics**. Like trying to identify keywords or tags for a blog, pulling out the topics, and even specific characters, in your book can lead you to new audiences and venues. Since my protagonist began birding as a child, I give talks about the importance of nature education for

kids at family-oriented programs. A restaurant I included in one book happily hosted a signing for me, and displays my books in a prominent place. HINT: Does one of your characters run a small business? Your local Rotary Club or Chamber of Commerce might be delighted to have you come speak to them about how that plays into your novel. Many groups are eager for new ideas and personalities to book for their meetings. Find a link between them and your work, and you've got a foot in the door.

2. **Research opportunities**. What groups in your community need speakers? My current goldmine is senior living communities who have busy activity calendars for their residents. Since many of my readers are older and enjoy birdwatching, speaking at these venues is a perfect fit for me. I've learned that many communities have on-site book clubs, too, and having an author (you!) available to join a gathering can mean a shortcut to your book being selected for reading. HINT: Would you be willing to talk to a high school class about something related to your book? Teachers are generally thrilled to have a guest speaker, and while you may not make any sales in the classroom, you can bet on word-of-mouth publicity (and perhaps a small fee from the school field trip budget!).

3. **Pick up the phone**. Nothing beats personal contact when it comes to booking events at creative venues. Find the right person to ask (research on the internet or by phone) and prepare a short, convincing, sales pitch as to how they'll benefit from your visit. Offer to email your photo, a brief bio, and talk description for

their use in promotion. Take your bookmarks to hand out, and books to sell and sign.

SIXTY-NINE

How to Plan a Multi-Author Cross-Promotion Event

Melissa K. Norris

Every writer I know feels pressure to build their platform. From the pre-pubbed stage, sending out proposals to an agent, then editor, to published authors working on keeping their numbers up, it can be a constant maze of hunting through websites telling you how to do it the best way.

Despite how you package promoting, be it in a contest, giveaway, or ad, there is only one thing that truly matters to determine its success. Are you giving your target audience something they find of value?

Notice I didn't say something valuable to a reader. There are many readers out there, but not all readers are your target audience. You need to have a deep understanding of your reader before you plan any promotional event, especially a multi-author one.

1. Start by identifying other authors who have similar target audiences or readers to yours. For cross-promoting to work, the audiences must be linked by a similar interest.

2. Decide what will be the common theme for the event. You'll need to decide before inviting the other authors to your event what the theme or purpose will be. And it is not to sell books. This is what you hope will be the end result, but the purpose of the event will be to somehow reach readers and enrich their time spent with you.

3. Send out the invites with a timeframe for response at least two months before the date of the event. Expect to have some authors not be able to join you. Be gracious and thank them for considering. Move on to the next authors on your list.

4. Ask for ideas or comments on how to make the event better. Allow the other authors to have a say in the event, but be sure you have one person who is the leader. When planning the "Mountain Hearth Christmas" event with four other authors, it was my original idea to just have it be a virtual cookie recipe exchange. Amanda Dykes had the idea of incorporating the printable Bible verses for garlands and or gift tags.

5. Be very clear on what is expected of everyone. While all of the fabulous authors in the Mountain Hearth Christmas worked together, it's best to let everyone know what you'd like them to do. For example: everyone is expected to share links on their social media pages each day of the hop, not just the day it's being hosted on their own website. Cross-promoting only works if everyone helps.

6. Send out reminders leading up to the event. The leader should send out reminders as things draw nearer. Keep them short and to the point. Always be respectful of others' time. Three weeks before, two weeks before, and the day before are a good time frame. You may want to have the leader send out daily emails the morning of the event with the link to that day's highlighted article and composed social media updates for people to copy and paste if pressed for time.

SEVENTY

Multiple Author Events—Yes or No?

Jan Dunlap

As a writer, the weight of book promotion falls on my own shoulders. Since that gets tiring, I'm always looking for ways to maximize the results of the events I do: my current goal is to market smarter, not just harder.

So when a writer friend told me about the great attendance and good sales she experienced at a multiple author event at a book store, I decided to give it a whirl with both of my book lines. That meant gathering other authors who've written about dogs (so I could promote my girl-meets-dog memoir *Saved by Gracie*) and collecting another crew of authors who've written about birds (to expand the audience for my fictional series, *Birder Murder Mysteries*).

This is how it played out:

National Dog Day. I broached the idea for a National Dog Day Night to a local independent bookstore, and they jumped at the concept! I offered to recruit authors to attend, and the store agreed to stock the books, set up chairs and a microphone, and do publicity. They even partnered with a local dog rescue group for more publicity and support. Luckily, three well-known writers with dog books live in my area, and they readily agreed to participate. We all thought it was a smokin' idea . . . but only five people showed up. What went wrong? Personally, I attributed it to the lovely summer weather; I myself would have chosen to be outside with my own dog, rather than inside with authors.

My big score, though, came from meeting the other authors, one of whom asked for an excerpt from my book to run in her monthly newsletter that goes out to thousands of readers. I made a hot contact even if the event fizzled.

For the Birds Night. I took this idea to a local Barnes & Noble and again, the events manager thought it was a winner. This time, it was a monumental headache for me to pin down the authors—talk about a flighty bunch! Not that any of them are absent-minded—it just took me a while to catch all these bird-chasing authors between their travels and professional obligations, not to mention the multiple email addresses so many of them use. I managed to round up five of the original ten that I contacted, and even then, I had one drop out at the last minute due to health issues, and one drop in who'd forgotten to confirm with me months earlier.

The event itself, though, was a big hit! We had over 20 people attend, a lively discussion ensued, and every author was signing several books by the end of the evening. Our B&N hostess invited us back for a spring event, and said her district manager had expressed interest in us taking our event to other stores.

After organizing two group events, my conclusion is that it's worth the effort in terms of both book promotion and author networking. Upfront sales might be disappointing, but as one more tool in your marketing toolbox, I highly recommend giving it a try.

And keep some aspirin handy.

SEVENTY-ONE

Preparing for a Radio or Podcast Interview, Part I

Anita Agers-Brooks

I'm not sure where you are on your writing journey, but if it hasn't happened yet, hopefully it will one day soon: Your invitation to be a guest on a radio program.

With the release of my book, *First Hired, Last Fired — How to Become Irreplaceable in Any Job Market,* I've done several interviews now, while working to line up numerous others.

Imagine my surprise when the podcast host for Engaging Life and Leadership called. Podcasts are internet radio shows, so they enable you to reach global listeners versus a regional audience. Think of it like this: Podcasts are the big-city landscape of audio, while most traditional radio programs have a home-town community feel. Each has its strengths and weaknesses, and each reaches different wants and needs.

Since my guest spot on Engaging Life and Leadership went over so well, I was asked to return—again and again. It didn't take long until the unexpected happened.

"Will you join the show as a permanent co-host?" Darren Dake asked.

We've now recorded over twenty episodes as a male/female team, discussing relevant answers for Christian men AND women in 21st century leadership. At last count, we are reaching 17 countries.

But why did I just tell you all of this? For a few reasons actually.

1. As authors, there's constant pressure to build your platform. From the beginning, I've trusted God to design mine, and partnered with Him in the building. He continues to do more than I could possibly have imagined.

2. The nail-biting prospect of guesting can terrify the most confident of men or women. So I want to share what has helped me survive small, nationally syndicated, and global radio programs.

Here's my pre-show routine:

- In Michael Hyatt's amazing **Get Published!** program, he advises the creation of a briefing book as a guide during your interview. I created a PDF synopsis of my book, including the questions sent to the host in the media release. If you'd like a copy of mine as a sample, feel free to email me at anita@anitabrooks.com. (Half of the hosts never asked the arranged questions, but my briefing book kept me on track when they strayed.)

- Double-check dates and times (accurate time zones especially) to ensure I don't experience a faux pas, and either scramble last minute or extend my nerves and frustration from a longer wait. My worst fear? Missing the opportunity altogether.

- Get a good night's sleep the night before. I've discovered half a Melatonin is a great way to enhance my natural sleep rhythm, providing deeper rest.

- Walk or exercise prior to my interview, making sure I finish an hour before show time.

- I take a shower about forty-five minutes before to freshen up.
- Share my prayer need on social media. Friends and family appreciate the chance to support me in advance. (Plus it reminds some who want to listen in.)
- About fifteen minutes before, I get prostrate in prayer. Literally. I lay on my living room floor, as flat as possible, and humble myself before God. I ask the Holy Spirit to guide my words and still my tongue when appropriate. He hasn't failed me yet.

In Part II, I'll list the things I do *during* the interview to help me spread the message in a more effective way. Some are plain old common sense, but a couple will surprise you.

SEVENTY-TWO

Preparing for a Radio or Podcast Interview, Part II

Anita Agers-Brooks

You may not think this pertains to you, but if you are an author, or aspiring author, there is something you need to face. One day, if you are fortunate, you will sit on the other side of a mic or telephone, answering questions from a show host. And you want to shine as brightly as possible, so your message connects with more people in the listening audience.

In Part I, I talked to you about preparing *before* the interview. This time, I want to share how I prepare *during* a radio or podcast episode.

I've gotten experienced in the process, and learned several things along the way. I'm going to tell you what happens behind-the-scenes that helps me do a better job. I hope this encourages and strengthens your confidence when it's your turn.

- **Here's the weird one, but I bank on it.** I make an interview tonic of raw, organic apple cider vinegar, raw local honey, a touch of garlic, and mix it into a glass of Appletini or Cherry Pomegranate Crystal Light. (No, I don't add alcohol, and I don't suggest it, no matter how tempting!) About five minutes before we air, I take two or three good swigs. It reduces phlegm, sore throat, a gravelly voice, and strengthens my tone when I speak. On commercial breaks, I'll sip a little more.

- **I have a fresh glass or bottle of water at the ready.** Keep anything you drink away from the microphone or telephone receiver—you don't want to gulp On Air. Word of caution: continue paying attention to what's being said or you might miss a question you need to answer. (Also I don't drink too much before the interview. If Mother Nature calls during the segment, it can get mighty uncomfortable.)
- **I place my briefing book in hand's reach.** (See previous post on what a briefing book is.)
- **I have a copy of my published book on hand.** During commercial breaks, I've had two hosts ask me to read a sentence or two directly from my own book.
- **Take slow, deep breaths** to reduce blood pressure and calm my nerves during breaks.
- **Listen twice as much as I speak**, making sure I don't cut the host off, or interrupt his/her flow. Remember, most people tune in because they like the host, or the program format. The percentage of audience members who listen due to the topic is small.
- **Strive to be myself**, while intentional about infusing a warm and welcoming tone to my voice. I imagine talking to a dear and trusted friend, even when the host is trying to stir a little controversy. I had this happen, and because I stayed calm and steady under pressure, allowing God's spirit to lead my response, it transformed the entire interview. By the end, the host was profusely inviting me back, and called my book fabulous three times. (I counted.)

- **When asked a challenging question**, I've found it's okay to say, "I'm not sure, I need to research or pray about it," or even to pause for a couple of seconds while crafting my answer. Adds a bit of dramatic effect anyway.

- **I follow the PIER method for engaging audiences** when I write and speak (Point, Example, Instruction, Reference). It ensures I maintain focus, interest, and credibility, while providing them with take-away.

Now, you're ready for your interview. It's your turn to shine—be brave, and go spread that message! This is what God called you for.

VII.

It Takes a Team

SEVENTY-THREE

Making Connections

Kariss Lynch

P ublishing is a funny beast. The author wears many hats—writer, editor, marketer, publicist, sometimes frazzled human being (all right, maybe it's most of the time). There are moments when the load seems overwhelming and I feel incapable of wearing every hat with excellence.

Marketing tends to be my weakest link. I'm passionate about my books, love to talk about them, enjoy sharing the story of God's faithfulness. But when it comes to selling the idea of why others should read them, I prefer to let people determine the quality on their own.

I know. I know. I'm still learning how to do this well. But the key is that I'm learning. Guest posts, social media, contests, etc. are all great tools that I am adding to my belt, but the most powerful tool in my arsenal is my network. These people fall into multiple categories, and every group is important.

1. Close friends and family. You've got to love this group. They are your biggest fans and cheerleaders. Occasionally they may be more biased than constructive with their feedback, but enjoy the affirmation. They've watched the journey, battled the insecurities and joy with you, and want to celebrate the finished product.

2. Fringe friends and acquaintances. These are the people familiar enough with you to ask about the book every

time they see you. They are also the ones who bought the book out of curiosity and support and are excited to watch the journey from a distance. If they love the story, you better believe they will share with their friends and family.

3. <u>Unknown readers.</u> These are the people whose constructive opinion you can count on most. If they love the book, then job well done. They hail from all over the country, sometimes out of the country, and their word of mouth is powerful. They don't know you, but love the heart in your books and will shout it from the mountaintops and anxiously wait for the next book. I love networking with this group. Their excitement fuels my own.

4. <u>Critics and commentators.</u> These are your influencers, bloggers, Amazon comment critics, etc. I don't necessarily advocate taking their opinions as gospel. But often, they have a powerful voice in their particular online spheres. Learn what they love and what they don't, filter it to see if there is truth, and build on these admonitions in your next book.

5. <u>The unreached.</u> The good news is that with all these other groups on board, the unreached are now reachable. Diligently work to add this group to the fold. Build relationships with your readers. Write stories that people can't ignore. And don't grow discouraged. This is a journey, not a short-distance sprint. Growth happens over time, and it's exciting to see.

But there is one connection that is the most important: talking to the Master Storyteller. He knows your story intimately, and He alone can weave your network into something beautiful.

Prayer is powerful. In moments of frustrated marketing, I've prayed that the Lord will get Shaken and Shadowed into the hands of people who need to read them, despite my best efforts.

And He has.

Some of my favorite interactions from readers come from those who never heard about the book but wandered into a bookstore, loved the story, laughed, cried, and found hope in Christ. Every time I read one of these messages, I praise the Master Marketer. In spite of my best efforts, He is still placing these books in strategic places.

More than spinning a great story and growing my craft, I want to make an impact. And that only comes through surrendering my ideas in marketing to the One who knows best. I figure with Him at the wheel, I'll do what I can and let Him do the rest.

SEVENTY-FOUR

All Aboard the Creative Team Train!

Jan Dunlap

Unless you work with a co-author, the act of writing is indeed a solitary activity.

Selling your writing, however, is anything but. (Think book signings, audiences, store owners, readers, reviewers, friends, foes . . .)

And that's a good thing, because if you were the only person involved in marketing your book, you might never want to put pen to paper (or fingers to keyboard) ever again. A one-person sales force means when sales don't meet expectations, you're going to have to fire yourself. Then who will you talk to during writing breaks?

Yes, your publisher will be doing some of your selling, but that can range from simply listing your book in their catalog to assigning you a short-term publicist to whatever the big publishing houses do (which I understand is much less than they used to do!). If you want to drive your sales-train—instead of just being a passenger going along for the ride—you need to be the chief engineer, reaching out to all those folks and activities I listed above.

But as engineer, you also have another job besides sales manager: **you need to oversee the creative effort that goes into**

preparing the infrastructure upon which your promoters will depend.

You need your own creative team: a group of individual contributors who shine at what they do and share your enthusiasm for your writing projects. Yes, it's going to cost you some money, but I'm convinced it's worth the expense when you assemble the right team to get the sales prep done.

Here are the team members I couldn't do without:

Website designer. A professionally designed website is essential for communicating your brand and presenting yourself as a professional author and speaker. Find the designer who 'gets' you, because she'll come up with other marketing ideas for you to try. I confess, I put this one off for a long time, thinking my basic (but amateur) website was sufficient. My redesigned site offers me more ways to connect with readers, and offers readers more reasons to revisit the site.

Video producer. I've had two book trailers done, and I plan to do more in the future as I expand the ways I use them. Working with the same experienced producer saves time and effort – he has my stock materials on hand and a clear understanding of how I want to present my work. He also has a vested interest in my success, since his business grows from referrals.

Key local media contacts. I know the local newspaper staffs well, which means they pay attention when I send press releases. Many of them have contacts in the wider media community, as well, and they are generous with sharing information and ideas.

Social networking experts. I have the best in the business, because I subscribe to (and read) their newsletters and blogs. What I have learned from these gurus has rapidly added both depth and breadth to my social networking comprehension and usage, and their desire to help writers succeed is evident. My go-to sites are: Social Media Examiner, startawildfire.com/blog, Post Planner blog, socialmouths, and Michael Hyatt.

SEVENTY-FIVE

Seven Key Members of a Writer's Team

Christina M. H. Powell

It's not any one person. It's not any one coach. It's the team.
— Brian McBride

What is true in sports is also true in writing. Becoming a published writer involves assembling a team of talented individuals who will help you write the best book possible for your readers. Here are seven key members of a writer's team and the roles they play to help a book succeed:

1. **Beta Readers** – A beta reader is someone who will read and critique the three chapters of your book that you will include in your book proposal if you are writing nonfiction or the entire manuscript if you are writing fiction. You will use this feedback to improve your manuscript before sending it to a literary agent. Choose a person who loves books, belongs to your target audience, and understands how to give feedback on the big picture of your writing instead of bogging down circling typos.

Give your beta readers a time frame for completing their critique and clarify that your manuscript is confidential and should not be shared with others. A beta reader who is also a writer or who understands the publishing industry is ideal. Send your manuscript to multiple beta readers and pay close attention to feedback that is echoed by more than one beta reader.

2. **Agent** – Your literary agent presents your book to publishers and negotiates the sale. However, your literary agent often provides guidance and editorial suggestions before your book proposal is submitted. He or she knows the industry, so take the advice. After your book is published, your literary agent can provide marketing advice and help you develop your writing career.

3. **Editor** – Your editor helps you polish your manuscript to its final form, while also guiding you through the entire publication process—title selection, cover art, book design, copy editing, and choice of reviewers.

4. **Reviewers** – You will encounter three types of reviewers in the traditional book publishing process. The first set of reviewers, selected by your editor, provide feedback on your manuscript. You can take or disregard their suggestions when writing your final draft. However, their insights help you see your book with fresh eyes and learn how your readers might respond to certain passages. The second set of reviewers read the final manuscript and write short reviews for inclusion on the back cover of your book. You select these reviewers with input from your editor. The last set of reviewers are the readers who bought your book and decided to review it on Goodreads, Amazon, a bookstore website, or their blog. All reviewers are essential for the success of the book and the development of your writing career.

5. **Marketing Director** – Your marketing director will help your book find its way to readers. He or she will coordinate ad placement, mailing copies of your book to key influencers, and the work of a team of publicists. Touch base with your marketing director if you see a valuable opportunity for getting the

word out about your book. Coordinate your author efforts with the marketing plan your publisher develops for your book.

6. **Publicists** – Publicists may specialize in broadcast, publications or online publicity. If you are fortunate to have a publisher that has a team of publicists working to promote your book, they will arrange radio and podcast interviews and connect you with print and online opportunities to introduce readers to your book.

7. **Key Influencers** – Key influencers are the individuals who will receive an early copy of your book from your publisher. These individuals should connect with segments of your target audience and be able to create positive buzz about your book. Choose influencers across a wide geographical area and with characteristics that represent the breadth of your likely readers.

Other individuals may join the team to help you create a valuable book for your readers, but these seven key team members make up the core of your team as a writer. Appreciate the expertise that each team member brings, and build a good working relationship with all of them.

SEVENTY-SIX

Get Other Authors to Work for You (and do the same for them...)

Kathi Lipp

Left to their own devices, authors tend to be solitary creatures. The only problem? It's lonely out there for a writer.

I've found one of the best ways to have some longevity in this biz is to gather up your own little crew. A few authors who have a variety of gifts and talents to learn from, teach, and generally keep each other afloat when major publishing houses merge and panic sets in.

Another great advantage to having a network of other authors is the ability to build each other's platforms. Here are just a few of the ways I do that each month:

- Feature each other's new releases on your blogs
- Promote your writer friends' books in your e-newsletter
- Shout from the Facebook rooftops about their accomplishments
- Create events together
- Team up together on virtual book clubs
- Carry each other's books on your websites and on your book tables

All of these networking opportunities I take advantage of on a regular basis. But the most effective, platform-building networking I do is by referring (and being referred by) other speakers.

When I am already booked for an engagement, I have a few other speakers/authors that I refer to these groups. But, I even take it a step further. After a great event, I will pass on one or two of my favorite author's speaker packets to the meeting planner, telling them that they may want to consider booking these authors for their next big gig.

I only do this with other speakers I have heard and trust. Nothing can make your credibility go south quicker than a bad referral.

The flip side of this is that I have other authors who pass my name along when they are done with an event. There is nothing better than great "word of mouth" given to a happy client.

I have had great results with this idea, and an added bonus: I have developed a great network of friends who go through this business with me. It is great to have someone to talk with who understands this sometimes very strange industry.

Action Plan:

- Hook up with a couple of speakers that you know and trust, and ask them if they would be willing to recommend you, because you would love to recommend them. (If you need speaker training, be sure to check out Toastmasters.org, CLASSeminars, or Proverbs 31 Ministries.)
- Create a speaker packet for your speaking ministry
- Exchange speaker's packets with your favorite author to hand out after your event

- Put a list of other speakers on your website in case you're not available to do an event

Feature another speaker/author in your monthly e-newsletter (and have them give away a couple of copies of their latest book) with a link to their speaking page

SEVENTY-SEVEN

How to Find Your Best Influencers

Jan Dunlap

The longer I'm in the writing business, the more I appreciate the importance of influencers in helping me build my audience and increase sales. What's tricky for many writers, however, is figuring out just who and where those influencers can be found.

Unfortunately, after eight years and eight books of being a published author, I still don't have a magic formula for identifying and recruiting those valuable assets for my marketing efforts. All I can offer you is my own experience and insights, so here goes:

1. It's great to have **known experts** or writers give you an endorsement for your book, but unless they are truly excited about your book and **independently give it exposure in their own networks**, the endorsement is just nice copy for your back cover, and won't produce momentum in sales. Those experts are busy with their own marketing and projects, and the truth is, they give endorsements widely as a courtesy, rather than out of commitment to your publicity goals.

2. The best influencers have **a stake in your sales**. Although my books sell around the world, my strongest

sales come from a local gift shop because the store owner enjoys my books so much, she talks them up to customers and regularly features them in store promotional materials. Because of her enthusiasm, I've had more press coverage in local media than I could procure by my own efforts and a consistently growing word-of-mouth readership. As an influencer, she's one of my best!

3. You need to continually **cultivate relationships with potential influencers**. This means reaching out via social networking and/or physically traveling to meet people in your field of interest who might find your books of value in their own professional goals. To market my girl-meets-dog memoir, *Saved By Gracie*, I make a point of connecting with animal rescue groups/animal humane societies online, and when possible, I attend their conferences/events as a vendor. I often give free copies to keynote speakers or other passionate animal lovers I meet, in hopes they will read and enjoy the book so much, they will mention it to others. Yes, this is basically a hit-or-miss method, but so far, I've always made a few excellent contacts and found one or two awesome influencers at such events. It's well worth my time and money to break into a new group of potential reader-buyers.

Connect with **bloggers with big audiences** in your target market and ask to send them a copy of your book in return for a review. Offer them additional copies to use as giveaways when they publish a review of your book, or whenever they might have a contest going on. Doing this gives you a reach well beyond your own social networks and local geographic area. I've met several significant influencers in this way, and they continue to give me promotional value with each new book.

SEVENTY-EIGHT

What the Apostle Paul Might Have Said About Marketing

Shellie Rushing Tomlinson

Looking for marketing help, dear writer? Why, you're in luck! Step right up to the internet and tell old Google what you need, but be prepared to stay a while. A plethora of reading material and marketing advice abounds online, addressing the subject from every imaginable angle–and then some.

Except, perhaps for this one: **Don't overlook the value of marketing your neighbor's work.**

Hear me out before you write me off (weak pun apology). I'm convinced that this would be the type of advice the Apostle Paul might have offered had he ever taught a class in Marketing #101. In God's School, the way up is down. Or, as Paul said in Philippians 2:3, *"Do nothing out of selfish ambition or vain conceit. Rather, in humility value others above yourselves."*

Yes, it's challenging to understand how to apply those holy words to our writing lives. Especially when we're constantly reminded that our platforms are everything and publishers find us only as attractive as our last sales numbers. But if God's word doesn't apply to all of our lives, it applies to none of it.

Selfish ambition is building our platforms with tunnel vision to the work of everyone around us.

God's way is to step away from my work long enough to value yours.

It's a valuable principle of marketing. I once thought I stumbled across it accidentally, but I now believe it has been entirely by God's design. He orchestrated it through my work as a radio talk show host when I began reserving a segment of time to interview other authors. In the early days of All Things Southern LIVE, these were authors I met during my travel—until publicists began discovering this new venue and pitching their clients' work.

I need to say this: I don't promote everything that comes across my desk. Sadly, this is often a matter of pure time constraints. I don't have the air time to interview even half of the authors whose galleys find their way to my desk. At other times, it's a matter of my personal reading preferences or my understanding of the reading habits of my listeners. However, for these very reasons, when I do read something that entertains me, challenges me, encourages me, or flat out stretches me, I'm able to bring it to my listeners with authentic excitement. My audience knows this, so they trust my recommendations.

So, how does this help my marketing efforts? Well, that's the beautiful thing. God's way is always a win-win. Over and over I've seen how celebrating the works of others rebounds to bless my own career.

We've all been told to build a reader base and encourage that connection by staying in touch. We also know how distasteful it is to promote our own work. Introducing other authors to our readers–when we're genuine about their work–allows us opportunities to stay engaged and interact with our communities in a natural way. In turn, our relationship with those authors invariably leads to our introduction to their readers.

Now that is marketing we can all manage. Can I get a witness?

VIII.

Tips & Tricks

SEVENTY-NINE

Stupid Marketing Tips

Krista Phillips

So, here I was.

Sitting here, trying to think of a fabulous post about marketing books.

The thing is, the "m" word tends to bring up fabulous pictures in my head of those middle of the night moments when one of my children come to me, saying, "Mommy, my tummy hurts—" then proceeds to vomit all over my side of the bed and floor, at times giving me and my PJs a good dousing as well.

I, uh, am not the biggest fan of marketing, if you can't tell.

I take that back. I LOVE the *idea* of marketing. I KNOW it is needed and I LOVE the byproduct of it: my books being known by people and being PURCHASED by people.

Maybe it just brings back bad middle school memories of trying to get people to like me when I was a pimple-faced, slightly overweight, four-eyed and teeth-gapped teenager ... the thought of trying to get people to like my books (thereby, it feels like, ME) still creates that knee-jerk reaction to curl up on my bed with chocolate and a romance novel to take me to another place.

But enough about my traumatic teen years.

Marketing is hard for a LOT of writers. Maybe we can WRITE some fantastic marketing copy, but getting out there and trying to peddle books out of our comfort zone is HARD!

(Those of you who find it super easy . . . feel free to market mine too. I won't mind!)

But in putting ourselves out there, it's also common to get tripped up by some really BAD marketing ideas, in an absence of good ones.

I remember when I first started researching publishing back in 2007 after I'd completed my first novel. I was searching online tips for getting an agent/editor to look at your book. One place touted the value of STANDING OUT in the slush pile. Print that proposal on colored paper! Use *FUN* fonts *with* **lots** *of* **bolds** *and* **italics**! Send goofy gifts that relate to your book in the mail to that editor. (one example was a baby shoe for a book about babies . . . ??) Make them be like, WOW, this person is really SERIOUS about wanting to be published!

I laughed, then decided I would probably NEVER be published because no way, no how, would I ever sink that low to use silly gimmicks.

Then I found a few agent blogs that suggested that when they got those out-of-the-norm proposals, they were immediately trashed for their stupidity.

PHEW!

The same goes with marketing. Creativity is a MUST, but sometimes in the name of creativity, we stumble on ideas that can be counterproductive.

Here are just a few things I've seen over the past eight-ish years I've been on this journey—that have made me NOT want to read a book.

1.) THE WORLD IS ENDING! THIS BOOK IS YOUR ONLY SALVATION! Maybe not those words exactly, but scare tactics or broad, unsubstantiated claims does not a good marketing plan make. "THIS BOOK WILL CHANGE YOUR LIFE

FOREVER." (Different than saying something a little more docile like life-changing fiction, etc) "GOD WANTS YOU TO READ THIS BOOK!" (Let HIM tell me that, thank you!) Sure, you might get some saps to buy it, but you probably won't find publishing success with this type of marketing for books.

2.) BUY MY BOOK (five minutes later) BUY MY BOOK (five minutes later) BUY MY BOOK (repeating 100 times per day!) Over-posting on social media is a hard one, because there is a fine line. We NEED to be bold and proud of our books and market them on social media, no doubt. However, tact is needed. When my Facebook newsfeed is filled with six different posts by the same author marketing the same book all in the same day? It's a good way to get yourself unfriended or at least blocked. Your Facebook marketing should draw people in, not annoy them.

3.) I MEAN, YOU DID BUY MY BOOK, RIGHT? Guilting people into buying your book is uncool. We all have different budgets and different reading tastes. I'll readily admit, there are some writing friends I have (who will remain nameless) whose books I haven't purchased Why? Partially because I'm a broke mom of four kids trying to make a living as a writer. HA HA! But also, I have my writing friends than I have time. The idea of marketing is to ENTICE them to read your book, not twist their arm.

4.) NOTHING. This is the stupidest idea of all. Just not doing anything because you're afraid of it. It's the one I'm most guilty of. Oh, I market, but I'll get an idea and think, 'Oh, no, that'd totally bomb' and move on. Just like in publishing, sometimes you have to fail a few (or a hundred . . .) times before you find that golden ticket/agent/editor/marketing scheme. But if you just sit back, cross your fingers and toes, and hope your books sell? Yeah. That is the WORST marketing idea of them all!

EIGHTY

Give 'Em What They Want, Not What You THINK They Want

Jan Dunlap

After fumbling around with social networking and reading every marketing article about it that I could get my hands on for the last year or so, I've distilled my promotional strategy down to a simple directive: **give readers what they want.**

I know that sounds obvious, but the tricky part is understanding the 'what,' especially once you realize that 'what' your readers want may not be the same 'what' that you THINK they want. The key is taking 'you' out of the picture, so you can clearly see your reader without your own perspective distorting your vision.

It's like reflective listening—you want to reflect back what the other person is saying without putting your own spin on his words, so you hear clearly what he said, and not what you think he said. Quick example of doing it wrong: my husband said he wished he'd taken music lessons when he was a kid, so I got him music lessons for Christmas. Two weeks into the lessons, he told me he didn't want to continue.

"But you said you wished you'd taken lessons as a kid," I reminded him.

"As a kid, yes," he said. "But now I have other interests that I'd rather spend my time on. You interpreted my comment as a current wish, which it isn't."

Ouch. I should have gotten him the shop-vac he said he needed, which I thought was boring.

Same idea applies to your readers.

Pay careful attention to what they say, or in the case of social media, what they really like to see and with what they engage.

For instance, I thought that as an author, I should be posting on Facebook about my WIP or upcoming events. Those posts, I've found, get little notice.

But if I post a photo of me getting kissed by a French bulldog, or a goofy homemade video of me singing (badly) about the cold weather, I get comments galore. Clearly, on Facebook, at least, my writing news is not very interesting to my readers.

Writing news is appreciated very much, however, by my newsletter subscribers, so that's where it now goes, along with on my website. As for LinkedIn, I post both events and business-related material, such as when my books get a rave review or included in an industry-recognized blogger's post.

For Twitter, I post quick links to interesting material in my subject areas (birds, nature, dogs, humor) or retweet entertaining posts, because I've found that those kinds of communications are most appreciated by my followers. Because it's a fast and short exposure, I tend to use Twitter more than any other social media platform as more of a shotgun approach—post and hope it spreads wide and far to get my name in front of a greater number of people, because that's the first step to finding new readers.

My experience has convinced me that connecting with readers, followers, and networks is a necessary piece of expanding my readership, but once I've reached new folks, it's time to shift gears and use social media to build relationships, not solicit sales.

That's why it's called social media, and not the shopping channel. Remembering to give the reader what they want is easy when it's the same thing you want to give your friends.

EIGHTY-ONE

Your Friends in the Book Marketing Business

Kimberly Vargas

Book marketing can be rather overwhelming, especially here in the middle of the publishing revolution. The good news is that there are more and more emerging companies out there who bring a lot of light to this dark arena. Whether you are an author looking for assistance or a reader trying to find the best deals available, this post is to create a compilation of resources you may find helpful.

Author Marketing Club: An author member can submit books for promotional opportunities, as well as access free online training and resources related to book marketing. A reader member will get notified about new and discounted books, and can discover new authors. This service is free for both authors and readers. You can upgrade to the Premium program if you wish for additional benefits, but it is not required for you to do so. Some of the options offered under a Premium membership include an Amazon book reviewer tool that can help you find reviewers who focus on your literary genre. www.authormarketingclub.com

BookBub: The best marketing dollars I have ever spent have been with BookBub. BookBub is a free daily email that notifies you about deep discounts on acclaimed e-books. You choose the types you'd like to get notified about—with categories ranging from mysteries to cookbooks—and they email you great deals in those genres. BookBub features e-books ranging from top-tier publishers to critically acclaimed independent authors. During my last campaign with BookBub, I spent about $260.00 and yielded thousands of downloads as a result. If you are looking for new readers, do yourself a favor and check out BookBub: www.bookbub.com.

Other great resources for readers:

Pixel of Ink: A website that features daily publishing of Free Kindle Books and Hot Deals. On any given day, there are *thousands* of Free Kindle Books available. www.pixelofink.com

Inspired Reads: The best Christian Kindle books on a budget. www.inspiredreads.com

Kindle Daily Deal: The best deals available for Kindle. www.amzn.com/KindleDailyDeal

EIGHTY-TWO

How to Make Your Readers SUPERfans!

Jan Dunlap

When you have a book published—be it in print or e-book—you want to get as much publicity as possible to sell copies, right?

Right!

Do your fans know this?

Well, yes, I think they do.

You THINK they do?

Here's my suggestion: **tell them you need their help** to generate that publicity. You need their word-of-mouth to help your book get launched amidst the thousands of books that are available.

You need to give them the **3 Rs of superfans: Read, Review, and maybe most importantly, Rave!**

With the launch of my newest suspense novel, *Heaven's Gate*, I put together a launch team of thirty readers who agreed to read and post a review on amazon.com and whatever other social networks they had, along with any word-of-mouth recommendations they might be able to give. Like many writers, I'm not especially fond of online marketing because it takes a lot of my time, but the fact is, writers in the 21st century need to cultivate their presence on it. (I, personally, have had varying success with different networks, but I continue to learn and work at it because I've seen its value at different times. Let's face it, if there's a gathering of readers anywhere—even online—don't you think an author would be remiss to ignore it?) What I've discovered since my book debuted last month, however, has added another piece to my formula of reading and reviewing: **you need readers to RAVE about a book to influence others to buy.**

So far, maybe this seems evident to you, but this next comment might catch your attention: I learned that **you need to tell your readers what to write.** I don't mean give them a script— you want their honest reaction. But what you need to do is **empower your readers to write raving reviews**, which result from two things: an awesome reading experience (which you have crafted with your book!) and a vocabulary that will reinforce what you want them to say.

Simply **suggest key words** you'd like your reviewers to use.

At first, I felt odd suggesting words to my readers to use in constructing their reviews. Then I realized that key words are ... well ... key. Keys, actually, to triggering the all-important call-to-action that every author needs to make to potential readers: You Need To Buy This Book Now. And guess what? Your reviewers are often very grateful to have your suggestions, because they want to write a strong review for you, but are often lacking in promotional experience and don't know how to best help you with their review. I asked my reviewers to use the words *suspense, Archangels series, faith and science, String theory, fast ride,* and *thriller.* They did, and as a result, the reviews for *Heaven's Gate* present a consistent rave of being a book you can't put down, which has cued new readers to order the book.

Remember, your fans want you to succeed. Making it easier for them to help you is the least you can do!

EIGHTY-THREE

10 Strategies to Keep You Afloat in the Treacherous Social Media Waters

Janalyn Voigt

What's a writer to do? Publishers expect you to connect with readers online, but new networks spring up before you can learn what to do with the old ones. New invitations arrive daily in the various inboxes you don't have time to check. You're tweeted, emailed, and updated out, and never mind all the invitations you have no time to decline. It's a slow-drip torture.

If the treacherous waters of social networking are swamping your ship, you're not alone. A wise writer fights back with a strategy. Here are ten strategies to help you:

1. **Pick your battles.** Decide where to focus your energy online. Although Facebook, Twitter, and LinkedIn have a greater share of traffic, your results may vary, depending on the audience you want to reach, your brand, and your particular style of networking. Pay attention to where your visitors come from, and you'll be able to make an informed decision about where to focus your efforts.

2. **Set aside specific times or a time limit for social networking.** Decide where and when and how you'll interact online and stick to your guns. Failing to approach the internet with this mindset makes it far too easy to lose track of time. If you have trouble adhering to a set time, use an egg timer or other alarm to warn you when your time is up.

3. **Manage your social networks from one dashboard.** I use and recommend hootsuite.com for posting to and tracking my social sites. With Hootsuite, I can post the same update to more than one site simultaneously and pre-schedule or auto-schedule updates. Another popular option is Tweetdeck.

4. **Use browser extensions to shortcut social tasks.** I favor Google Chrome because of the extensions I can add to my browser. I use Silver Bird to post to Twitter, check my tweet stream, follow search terms and hashtags, and for alerts when I'm mentioned on Twitter—all from my browser. I use Hootsuite's Hootlet, Bitly (a link shortener that tracks stats), Google+, Facebook, LinkedIn, and Stumbleupon extensions as well. Pinterest's Pin It button is a big time-saver. All of these tools operate from small icons embedded at the top of my browser. This cuts down my visits to the social sites themselves, saving a tremendous amount of time.

5. **Understand your brand and how it applies to your social networking efforts.** If you don't know who you are and what you have to offer, you won't know what to build and can spend a lot of time investing in the wrong thing.

6. **Know your audience.** Understanding who you're writing for and what they care about is an essential step in developing an effective social media strategy. Make the effort to discover and develop your target audience.

7. **Develop tunnel-vision and wear blinders.** When you log into a social site, distractions abound. Keep your focus. It can help to follow a simple list. Here's an example for Facebook: respond to comments and post to my wall, post to three friends' walls, upload a picture, check emails, accept or decline new friends, respond to event invitations, and log off (30 minutes).

8. **Adhere to a social media schedule.** I've programmed Google Calendar to send me email reminders to pay more attention to one social site over others on a specific schedule. During these visits, which occur weekly, I do maintenance tasks like revamp my bio, check that my links are current, swap out my profile picture, upload videos, make sure my site adheres to my brand, and the like.

9. **Count the opportunity costs.** Time spent on social sites is time not spent doing other things. It's easy to get caught up by online friendships to the detriment of real-life relationships. Reminding yourself of your priorities helps you switch activities or power down the computer.

10. **Track yourself online.** Install Rescue Time to track you online and send you productivity reports. If you lack discipline, this software can help you find it again. There are even options you can set to restrict your internet access at certain times.

I rarely spend more than half an hour a day on social networking, and often considerably less, but for the most part I cover the bases. I hope you can glean from the strategies that have kept me sailing away on SS Social Media.

EIGHTY-FOUR

Profits from Back-of-the-Room Sales

Becky Johnson

Let's be honest, most work-horse writers cannot make a living by advances alone. However, if you combine writing with speaking and profitable back-of-the-room sales, look out! Writing, speaking and book/product sales is a true triple whammy, each avenue supporting the other. Each leg of this career stool brought in roughly one-third of my income. Here are some ideas for a money-making book table.

Bundle or Bag 'Em

Bundle items into gift bags. For example, I would put my humor books for moms in clear gift bags with a pretty sheet of tissue paper and call it "Laughter Rx for Moms." I created another bag I called "Smiles for the Stressed-Out Soul" that included my books on slowing down and thriving. People want to give their friends some tangible love, so selling your books in gift bag form makes them instantly ready to share.

Something for the Kids

I wrote four books for young kids (*Gabe & Critters*) and five "first chapter" books for ages 7-11 (*Camp Wanna Banana*). Moms and grandmas love to buy something for children. I found darling finger puppets, cute plastic "bookworms," and small plush spider monkeys that tied in with the books' themes. The eye appeal of colorful items surrounding the books proved irresistible. It took time to find items that were lightweight, small, fun, sturdy, and profitable. But when I did, books flew off the children's section of my table.

Offer a Bargain

In what I now view as a great business opportunity, two of my books went out of print. I negotiated to buy a literal truckload of them for 72 cents each. I bought 10,000 books and filled up an empty guest room, wondering what in the world I had done. However, I sold every book by offering them "2 for $5.00" to retreat attendees. A profit for me, and a great deal for them. The event planner put a coupon in the retreat bags for this "special bargain," ensuring a rush to the book table.

High Profit Items

I quickly discovered that women wanted to take my "retreat talks" home or share with a friend. So I had audio CDs made of my talks and called them "Girlfriend Getaway." I sold four talks for $15.00. My investment in the CDs (including case) was only $3.00 each. Many speakers create their own workbooks or study guides to go with their books and make a nice profit.

Mention in Your Talk

I am turned off by speakers who hawk their books like an infomercial. I've found it much more natural to say, "In my book, *Worms in My Tea*, I told a story about a time when . . .", then simply tell the story. People would always show up at the table asking for the book that contained the story I told.

The More Books, Higher Profit

The greater the variety of books you have on your table, the higher the profit; however, you don't have to author all the books you sell. If you refer to books by other authors in your speeches, negotiate with a publisher to buy them in bulk at a good discount and sell them on your table. Or sell other product-tie-ins. If you wrote a cookbook, you might sell adorable aprons. If you teach writing classes, you might offer pens and blank journals that have fun literary themes.

Information Sheet for Event Planner

In a packet of information that I would mail ahead or email to the event planner, I included a Book Description Sheet. It had the picture and title of each book with a one or two sentence description below it. This would help volunteers get quickly familiar with the products. Always ask for at least two volunteers to help with the book table, giving them free books as a thank you. After you speak, women will want to chat and have you sign books, so having others take care of the money exchange is essential.

Bookmarks

Create a cute bookmark to be tucked into the books you sell on your table with information leading to your website, other books, etc.

Signs & Set Ups

I typically only put about ten copies of each book on the book table at a time, re-filling it from a box under the table as they sold. Make clear concise signs to prop up on your table that clearly show the price of your books. Go for visual clarity rather than cuteness. And be sure to take credit cards; it greatly increases sales.

I hope these tips prove helpful to you and increase your profits as you speak and write.

EIGHTY-FIVE

Marketing with Integrity: Five Tips on What Not to Do

Gillian Marchenko

Most writers prefer to focus on craft instead of marketing. But let's face it. These days, authors need a platform to jump from in the publishing world. Without flexing the mammoth muscle of the internet, our publishing goals may not materialize.

Humph.

I'm new in the business. I've written a memoir about having a baby with Down syndrome while living as a missionary in Ukraine. I've landed an agent. I now participate in the shaky step of pitching my project to editors.

And I've already committed marketing blunders.

Here are five tips on WHAT NOT TO DO in marketing.

1. Don't use your kids to get 'likes.'

After my amazing agent Sarah Joy Freese encouraged me to attract more likes on my Facebook Fan page, I went a little nuts. I hosted a giveaway on my blog in exchange for Facebook likes and Twitter followers. I then convinced my four children to write and perform a "likes rap" video. They were cute. It was fun. It killed an afternoon at our house.

Giveaways and videos are great marketing tools. But I went overboard. I posted the video, and re-posted, and re-posted until my kids were even tired of watching themselves perform. My idea morphed into a "look at me" festival until a friend sent me a gentle message saying, "Really, Gillian? This isn't you."

2. Don't spam.

Spam is no longer just canned pork.

According to About.com, "Spam is any unsolicited commercial advertisement distributed online." If you post links repeatedly on social media without engaging in community and conversation, you may be considered a spammer and people are going to find you annoying.

3. Don't just ask. Give.

It is better to give than to receive. Let's face it. People don't care about us. Readers want a takeaway. They want perspective, a lighter mood, encouragement, escape.

In marketing, it is essential to give. Share links. Retweet. Interview people on your blog. Ask questions on your Facebook page. My writing tribe is best formed through reciprocal interaction and authentic interest.

4. Don't market without a plan.

My marketing blunders have stemmed from too much excitement and lack of preparation. At first, I had no marketing plan. It's difficult to have integrity at high-speed. Now, I try to step back and see the big picture. What marketing strategies will best utilize my schedule, gifts, and goals? I am no longer allowed to dream up an idea and run with it before a time of reflection, planning, and prayer.

5. Don't forget to write.

Marketing pursuits easily swallow work hours. When my time is not structured, I blog, tweet, update statuses, and read about marketing. But I might not write.

Thus enters the need for limits. Some writers allow a half hour in the morning and again at night. Others (insert ME!) require a little extra help. Turning off the internet is a great tip. Author Media, a website dedicated to help writers build their platforms, has a post providing seven apps that assist a writer's occasional lack of self-control. Consider checking it out!

EIGHTY-SIX

Taming the Marketing Monster

Jan Dunlap

When my daughters were little, they were convinced that a scary monster was waiting in the bedroom closet at night. Our solution was an easy one: I gave them a small hammer to put under their pillow, so when the monster came out, they could conk it on the head. Oddly enough, the monster never showed up, and my daughters slept soundly through the nights.

Empowerment is a wonderful thing.

Now that I've become a published novelist, I've discovered that most authors have a similar problem: there's a scary monster in our closets named Marketing, and it will come out of hiding even if you keep a hammer under your pillow. Not only that, but if you ignore it, Marketing will sneak out when you're not looking to destroy all your hard work to become published.

On the other hand, if you learn to tame it, Marketing will become your faithful friend, bringing you exposure, opportunities, and book sales. So instead of the hammer, here are a few empowering ideas to stick under your pillow tonight to help you begin the taming of your marketing monster.

1. **It's YOUR monster.** No one else is going to take responsibility for it, so you need to learn as much as possible about the feeding and care of it. Read blogs and

262 | BEST OF WORDSERVE WATER COOLER

books about book marketing. Create a list of media contacts in your area that includes radio stations, televisions, newspapers, magazines and even bulletin boards (find out who gives approval to use them!). Add the names of librarians, book store managers, and book club contacts. Make a roster of blogs that relate to your topic/novel where you can visit and leave comments. By creating your own database of ideas and contacts, the question of "what do I do?" becomes "where do I start?"

2. **Feed your monster every day**. Choose one marketing activity. Do it. Today. Write an announcement or press release of your book's publication and email it to your contact list. Visit five blogs and mention your book. Donate a copy to the library. Get a Facebook page. Don't worry about results at this point; just get the word out that you've got a book published. Tomorrow, choose another marketing task and do it. The next day, do the same thing. Feeding your monster a steady diet of small marketing activities will keep it content and much less scary. Over time, all those tidbits of publicity you've done will add up and begin to yield the bigger results you want: a growing readership.

3. **Take your monster out to play** on a regular basis. Meet other authors and network with them on marketing ideas and contacts. Plan joint events. Share experiences. Commiserate over the failures. Celebrate the triumphs. Laugh. Create your own marketing support group.

Most of all, don't let Marketing scare you. All it really wants is your attention...and to get out of that closet. You just have to open the door.

EIGHTY-SEVEN

Hope for Shrinking Violets

Rebecca L. Boschee

If you follow industry blogs, you've probably seen advice on how to promote your book or author brand.

You get it. You also probably know social networking is critical to self-promotion these days. If you know this, and you haven't yet jumped into the fray, could it simply be you aren't *comfortable* with it?

A Myers-Brigg personality study tells us half the U.S. population consists of **introverts.** Surprising, right?

Not really. You just don't always notice them next to the more conspicuous extraverts. Introversion isn't the same as being shy, though. It's a natural preference for solitude and reflection. We live in a fast-paced, "noisy" world that expects everyone to keep up. You see the conflict.

It's not hard to imagine a good number of writers cringe at self-promotion—not because they don't know what to do, but because the idea is emotionally draining to them. And maybe a wee bit nauseating

While introverts may have a harder time making small talk (hmm, Twitter?) or new friends (ahem . . . Facebook?), they do enjoy activities with long stretches of solidarity (writing, anyone?). If it makes you nervous to comment on a blog—if you write, edit, then rewrite your Facebook or Twitter posts—if you feel like you must say something witty or nothing at all—if it seems everyone else is having a grand old time with social media but you—you might be an introvert.

You're not alone. Heck, I'm there *right now*. But here's the thing about introverts—we're in our own heads a lot. We know if we want to succeed, we have to venture out of our comfort zone, like it or not. Fortunately, social media can work in an introvert's favor:

- Need time to process information? Great! Rather than being forced to think on your feet, participate in conversations at your own pace. Mull things over to your heart's content before you engage. Just don't get stuck there.

- Enjoy people but prefer them in small doses? Easy! All one has to do is Google to find a number of applications that allow future scheduling of pre-written updates for sites like Twitter, rather than facing them every day. Or, you could begin by engaging in a site you feel most comfortable with (GoodReads worked well for me), then feed your updates to Facebook or Twitter to help you appear more 'talkative' while remaining true to yourself.

- Trouble making small talk or accumulating friends? Start small. Like someone else's post. Retweet a relevant article. Share a link or a picture on tumblr. You don't have to talk much to say a lot. Just be sure you're being thoughtful about what you share—no problem for an introvert!

Remember, every move you make in the social media realm makes the next ones easier. The trick is to **get moving**.

EIGHTY-EIGHT

Marketing: To Do and Not To Do

Shelley Hendrix

I t isn't there. I looked," I told my mother so many times I lost count.

I also lost count of how many times she looked in the same place I did and said to me, with frustration in her voice, "Shelley, it's right here!"

Ugh. I hated when that happened. I felt stupid, embarrassed, and defective.

Why could SHE see it, but I couldn't?

It took a few years, but finally, by the time I was 10 or 11 years old, I learned to instead say, whenever I couldn't find whatever she said to look for or retrieve for her, "I don't see it." I'm 40 years old now, and I still use those same words in that situation.

What does this have to do with marketing? I'm certainly no expert in this field, but I have learned this: just because folks don't see our books, products, services, or goods, it doesn't mean they aren't there. It also doesn't mean they don't have value. It just means that sometimes people need help to see the good stuff right in front of them.

So, how do we do this in an already saturated market where everyone (and sometimes their pets!) are on social media, have a blog, and publish their work? (I kid you not about pets, either.)

I asked around, and want to share with you what other authors shared with me. I am confident these tips will help you (and me!) in the challenging world of marketing our writing in addition to creating the content we're trying to market.

Pay attention to social media: Don't discount the value of sharing some freebies with folks right where they are. Find out where your audience hangs out most on social media and focus the majority of your social media time and attention there. For example, my readers tend to be on Facebook more than Twitter, so while I am in both places, I don't kill myself in the Twitter-verse when more engagement happens on Facebook (and increasingly on Instagram and Pinterest).

Remember, as you engage in today's world of technology, these words from Marketing guru Rob Eagar:

"In a fast-paced world where Facebook, Twitter, and the 24/7 news media allow everyone to have a voice, it's more important than ever to cut through all the noise. Use power-bites to punch through the cacophony, gain people's attention, and spread your message like wildfire."

And this, from marketing expert Lori Twichell:

"The key to good marketing is making a connection with your audience. It's got to be genuine. People can see through selfish motives. If you are only there to promote your book or product, people can sense that." The more you get to know your audience and really make that honest contact, the more you'll end up with a loyal audience that will follow not just this book, but future endeavors as well. That's a key part of social media that is lacking in so many. We all love making new friends and connections, but no one wants to be spammed!

Newsletters: Emailing your subscribers is the best way to get content in front of your readers on a consistent basis. When they subscribe or give you their contact info, they've invited you to connect with them. Make sure to add value to your subscribers' lives, inviting them to open, read, and engage—be aware of what can feel "spammy" to your subscribers. In other words, don't just send emails to send emails. And make sure you give more than you request.

Here's another tip from Lori Twichell: "Tuesday, Wednesday, and Thursday are the best days to send newsletters. On Fridays people are eager to go home and clean out their inbox more quickly and on Mondays, they're buried in the weekend's email pile up."

Giveaways: Take advantage of what God has made available to you. What message has He entrusted to you to share with others? Offer some freebies along the way that build your credibility as one to listen and learn from in this over-saturated market.

As writers, we long to have readers find value in what we have to say, right? It can be so difficult to balance the discipline of learning and expressing with the necessity to also market what we write. Ultimately God is our greatest promoter. If we can remember that our social media numbers, our book sales, and our greatest accomplishments do not come close to God's power to promote us in due season, we'll remain at peace and loving life on the way to where we're going.

Marketing Like Your Favorite Authors

Rachel Phifer

I'd studied the writing blogs, so I knew when my novel released it was time to get busy. I lined up guest blogs, interviews and book reviews. I advertised on every social media site I could think of. My new website was up and running and I'd had a personal blog going for a few years. I spoke of the book to everyone I came across. I even hawked my book at a nearby fair. You want platform, I'd give you platform.

After a few months, I was exhausted. My introverted self felt raw after all of the exposure. And despite some great reviews of the book and a ton of five-star comments on Amazon, the book hadn't soared to the bestseller list. Actually, while it definitely had some fans, it hadn't picked up a lot of notice at all.

I wondered why I'd signed up for a writing career in the first place. I had a busy life with a full time job and a family. Who had time for all of this marketing, which by the way, was definitely not my forte? Marketing had taken so much of my time, I'd forgotten about the joy of writing fiction. Because of course, I wasn't writing fiction. I didn't have the time.

I began to study some of my favorite novelists and surveyed what they'd done as far as platform, and the answer was surprising. Almost nothing.

They all had websites of course. Lisa Samson started a blog, but stopped, saying the blog was stealing the creativity and time she needed to write. Dale Cramer and Athol Dickson blogged, but were invariably inconsistent, sometimes going a couple of months without a post. Davis Bunn's blog posts were regular, but were strictly announcements about his book events and reader praise. Penelope Wilcock writes hers like a diary, simply telling about searching for a lost cat or going to the dentist.

Sure, most writers did interviews and some guest pieces when a book came out. They did a few bookstore signings around the release and perhaps a speaking engagement or two in between. But they focused their time on what they were best at: writing amazing novels.

Because they were single-minded and purposeful about their fiction, they had output. They improved their craft. They built a readership.

No press in the world will help you if you're not writing new material, right? And yes, getting noticed is a bit random. Fantastic writers sometimes stay near the bottom of the midlist while so-so writers are household names.

But I've decided to follow my writer role models, best sellers or midlist. Yes, I'll do occasional blogging and other marketing. I've got my social media set up and will make some posts and connect to readers who contact me.

But in the end, I'm not a social media expert or a blogger or a speaker. I create story worlds and characters. I play with words. I edit what I've written until it's the book I'd want to read. It's what I'm good at and it's what I love. It's also what makes me a writer.

So this is the best marketing advice I've got, as backwards as it might seem: write more, write better.

IX.

The Bigger Picture

NINETY

Spiritual Marketing

Martha Carr

There are now endless marketing tips and tools available to everyone with every kind of budget. It has gotten much harder to know when to stay strong and push on through a marketing plan that's not quite working and when to let go and see what happens. It's a blessing and a curse for a writer.

I've been writing and publishing for a few years and I've been fortunate enough to get the chance to be traditionally published and to self-publish. I've had the chance to have no money for marketing and a healthy budget. The lessons I learned from the experiences have proved to be invaluable to my life as a writer but not in the way I expected, especially when it comes to marketing.

What I discovered has felt like an obvious answer and has given me back my love of writing. Years of frustration over marketing had slowly taken that from me till I wondered if I wanted to write anymore. That's when I paused and started listening from within and finally got an answer.

First, remember that when it comes to the actual writing, we all have a calling, an urge to write in one style or another and it's pretty difficult to get us to stray from it. Mine is to write a series of thrillers, the Wallis Jones series, that include big conspiracies and average families searching for a way to deal with it all. For some characters, the answer is God, while others keep searching, hoping for a different answer.

No matter how many times I went and tried another style of writing, I eventually came back to that mix.

Marketing, however, is altogether different, especially in a quickly changing world full of experts who say they can help sell your book. I've tried quite a few of them and with both good and bad results. In the end, it was all a lot simpler than I was trying to make it.

The answer was to live life on life's terms. In other words, if there's enough in the budget to do some marketing, then consult with the experts, weigh the options and set out with a plan. Keep the focus on the one plan and invite God into the entire process.

Instead of focusing on how many books were selling, my attention shifted back to what motivated me in the first place. I wanted to write because I had something to say. The fun returned because it was no longer about the outcome. So much of marketing can be about outcome if you let it.

That's where I've started using spiritual marketing as my guide and letting go of the results. My part is to just do the piece of marketing that's due today and then stop. I find myself sitting down to write without gritting my teeth or thinking about who might want to read it. I'd still like to sell a lot of books but my stomach doesn't lurch when someone asks me how many have sold and I don't feel compelled to hunt down opportunities.

I've got a plan in place for my next book, *The Keeper*, that is reasonable and in line with my current budget for time and money. Outcome is out of my hands and I turn it over daily to the one place I know will be able to do something with it. I do my part in all of it but I'm not making sure everyone else is also doing their job. Until I adopted the idea that God would need to be part of the marketing as well, it was never enough. But for me, spiritual marketing means God can get me wherever He wants me to be, so I can be assured this is my journey and relax into it.

NINETY-ONE

Marketing for the Introverted Writer

Janalyn Voigt

A ll you need is you, yourself," marketing expert and author James Rubart once said with regard to marketing. His comment, given at a meeting of Northwest Christian Writers' Association, stuck in my mind because I didn't believe him.

That's easy for you, Jim, I thought with a touch of asperity. *You are an extrovert who can walk into a bookstore and chat with the owner without breaking into hives.*

I am an introvert. If I had my way, I'd retire to a closet to write, coming out only to eat, sleep, and possibly notice the existence of my family. Okay, I'm exaggerating, but I really do have a closet office. My post describing it spiked visits to my website, which makes me suspect I'm not the only introverted writer. Welcome, and here are some of the lessons I've learned along the way.

- **Promoting is not nearly as hard as I was making it.** Once I busted through my own resistance and consistently marketed my book, I harnessed the power of routine. I was looking at the whole marketing puzzle at one time, but we really only solve a puzzle one piece at a time.

- **I don't have to be a social butterfly to effectively market a book.** All I need is the willingness to touch people using whatever format I find comfortable. That doesn't have to be face-to-face, necessarily. The internet allows me to promote to those I probably will never meet. As a writer, I'm wired to be a communicator, and communicators need listeners. That makes me a people person. Who knew?

- **Marketing is not the same as going to the dentist.** It can even be fun. Really. The key is to employ platforms that work well for you and that you enjoy or at least can tolerate. Your platforms can be in-person or online. Sometimes you need to compromise to attain a goal. For example, although I would rather not speak in public, if I want to fulfill my desire to teach other writers, I have to overcome my reluctance.

- **I can market with my writing.** I had a Hallelujah moment when I realized I could promote my book by writing related content for magazines, book sites (like Wattpad and Goodreads), or on my website as a subscriber incentive.

- **I don't have to be at every social site.** I have better results when I specialize at one or two sites rather than trying to keep up with them all. As a bonus, I have more time for writing.

- **Keeping track of people is important.** I confess. I lose people online. I don't mean to, but there are too many conversations with so many people. List the most important people to you as an author, and then make sure you engage with them on a regular basis.

- **Push past your fears.** This lesson was one of the hardest for me, and something I have to learn all over again on a regular basis. If I let fear stand in the way, I cheat myself of fulfilling my God-given calling. Not only that, but I deprive others I want to reach with my writing. In light of that, my fears don't seem quite so compelling.

Jim Rubart was right when he said that you only need you, yourself, to market your book. Don't worry about being someone you are not. Instead, use your talents to sing your unique song to those who need to hear it.

NINETY-TWO

The Business of You

Jeff Calloway

Social media is full of the white noise of people promoting themselves. Writers promoting books, ministry leaders promoting tools for church growth, singers promoting new releases, churches promoting their church, and on and on it goes. Tweets for how to lead your church, how to get more followers, how to make money off your blog. The list is endless. Social media has become a clogged highway of everyone promoting themselves and their newest content that will help you _____ (fill in the blank). The problem is, I have been pulled into this white noise that seems to get lost on the people who are seeing constant media feeds in Twitter, Facebook, Linkedin, Pinterest, Instagram, Google+, and the other social media sites.

What is a Christian to do when it comes to self-promotion in a me-driven world? As writers and artists, we produce content we believe others would benefit from consuming and implementing into their lives, ministries, or business organizations. Is it wrong or sinful for us as Christians to promote ourselves as writers, artists, pastors, and ministry leaders? The fine line we have to walk keeps some people from promoting themselves and their work. On the flip side, other believers promote themselves without shame and almost to the point of being obnoxious.

1. It's Not About You

Rick Warren popularized the statement "It's not about you" in his bestselling book *The Purpose Driven Life*. Even though we verbalize this thought and half-heartedly believe it, do we live it out when it comes to self-promotion? The way you live this out without putting yourself front and center is to focus on other people. When you tweet, FB, or use other social media, always make it about other people, not yourself. Put the focus on God, your spouse and family, other leaders, and people who have made an impact in your life.

2. Self-Promotion Is Not a Sin, But Can Become Sinful

Self-promotion in and of itself is not a sin, but when all the focus all the time is about you, it becomes sinful. While everyone wants to think they are agents of humility, that rarely is the case. Humility and pride are opposing forces in our lives. We believe that we are not prideful and have humble motives. But motive plays a part in this equation. Why are you promoting yourself? Are you looking to make a living? Wanting to become well-known?

God created the creativity that flows from your writing, your voice, and your speaking, and it can be used to provide financially for you and your family. Never should we promote the creative gift we have as ours and claim it as our own. God gave us the gifts we have to be shared with others, so they can enjoy and benefit from the content that flows from what we create.

Strive to be humble, *because God resists the proud, but gives grace to the humble.*

3. Your Identity Is Not in Success

Our culture values success in everything that we attempt to accomplish and there is nothing wrong with being successful. The problem comes when we worship success and when our identity is grounded in whether or not we achieve that success. Our identity, as followers of Jesus, is in Jesus. We should teach our children and others to be successful, but only in order to bring glory to Jesus. Athletes are often criticized for glorifying God when they are successful. What the critics do not understand is that those athletes know their success is not for themselves but for someone else.

If you look at my website (www.jeffcalloway.com), you see that I promote my writing and other endeavors I undertake. I struggle with self-promotion. It probably has to do with one's personality and experiences in life, but I find it distasteful sometimes that I toot my own horn. What about you?

NINETY-THREE

Entertaining Angels

Bob Welch

I've been marketing books of mine now for more than 20 years but only recently realized a big mistake I was making: Thinking it was only about books and sales.

Instead of, say, salt and light. Or experiences. Or giving instead of getting.

Example: I used to fret when I'd show up for an event and only a handful of people would be there. It made me feel like a failure. Like I was wasting my time and, given my poor-me attitude, the time of those who showed up.

Then it dawned on me: God must have some purpose for me to be wherever I was. And if people are important to God then they should be important to me, whether three or three hundred show up.

"I don't worry about the folks who didn't show up," I now tell people if there's a sea of empty chairs. "I'm just thrilled to be with those of you who did. Thanks for coming."

Changing my attitude changed everything. Realizing my worth is defined by God's love for me and not by any popularity I might get from people, I loosened up and had more fun.

Sure, I've had my *moments*, but, more often than not, I started laughing at situations that otherwise might have angered me. "OK, OK," I might say to a group of eight people amid twenty-

five chairs, "let's all scoot to the center to make room for others."
(Proverbs 18:12: Humility comes before honor.)

I became less concerned about selling books than about making sure people were having a good experience.

I became more attuned to others, reminding myself that perhaps there was just one person in the audience who needed some inspiration or a good laugh from me that day.

Recently, one event hammered home this lesson. In the spring I had set up an event at a small-town library regarding a new children's book I'd written and my friend Tom had illustrated. At the time, I had casually joked with the librarian that maybe we'd make it a barbecue.

Six months later—and three days before an event that I'd all but forgotten about—I got an e-mail from the librarian. "Can we help you at all with the barbecue Wednesday night?"

I called Tom. "I guess I sort of promised we'd do a barbecue for their town," I said.

He didn't say, "You WHAT?" He's way more grounded than I am. Instead, he said, "Let's do it, baby!" and organized who would bring what.

As I rolled down a freeway with a grill in the back of my '95 pickup, I said to myself: *Are we really putting on a barbecue in a town of 600 people?*

That's when I heard a thud. Despite my tie-down job, the grill had flipped over, its guts strewn around the pickup bed. It was 95 degrees. I was on the side of a freeway trying to re-secure a grill. And I was not happy. *Does John Grisham have to do stuff like this to sell a few books?*

Once Tom and I reached the town, 30 minutes away, nobody showed up. At first.

Then, slowly, people trickled in. Five. A dozen. More. Tom started grilling dogs. A group broke out in "Happy Birthday" to a friend of theirs. I realized people were having a blast.

A woman took me by the arm. "I brought my neighbor," she said. "She's dying of cancer and said she would love to meet you. She loves your writing."

Two hours later, in the pink light of an Oregon sunset, Tom and I were heading home when he said something I've never forgotten: "This was one of the coolest nights of my life."

Same here. We'd grilled and given away 48 hot dogs, sold two dozen books and brought together people in a small town for an evening of fun.

What's more, I'd had the privilege of spending time with a woman who would, three months later, be dead, but who somehow thought seeing me was important.

Now, I don't even like to call it "marketing." I call it a privilege to spend time with people—sometimes many, sometimes just a few—who think I'm important enough to give up a few hours of their time to see.

And I remember Hebrews 13:2: "Do not forget to show hospitality to strangers, for by so doing some people have shown hospitality to angels without knowing it."

NINETY-FOUR

Shameless: How to Fail a Book Signing (but Not the Writing Life)

Leslie Leyland Fields

"Art is born out of humiliation."
— *W.H. Auden*

I had a fantastically unsuccessful book signing in a big box store not long ago. (Yes, signings still occur, despite the take-over of social media.) Afterwards, licking my wounds, I turned to a book on my own shelves, *Mortification: Writers' Stories of Their Public Shame*. In it, Margaret Atwood, Rick Moody, Billy Collins and a constellation of such literary brights offer up the most companionable ignominies and embarrassments. (Fittingly, I bought the book used, online, for a penny.) My own parade of humiliations that night were paltry next to theirs. Still, couldn't I do better?

Two weeks later, an internet search on "book signings" confirmed my suspicions. According to several book signing experts, I did indeed do everything wrong. First, I missed the Webinar on "The Seven Steps to Turn Yourself into a Celebrity." In another article, I violated nearly every one of thirteen steps, beginning with, "Decide, in advance, what sort of clothing you want to be seen wearing by your reading public." (Did I do this? No.) Step #6 advised bringing along a printout of your manuscript for fascinated readers. (Really?) My most egregious error was the last step: my failure to inform the store managers that I would be the bookstore's official greeter while I was there. Nor did I walk around with several copies of my book introducing myself to everyone in the store, as he advised, pressing my own books and bookmarks into their astonished hands.

I would rather demonstrate the wonders of Balinese kitchen knives through the Christmas season at Walmart than resort to such tactics.

We all know we need to successfully promote our own work. But when we sacrifice leisure, sleep, money, and most costly of all, time with our families so that we can write, none of us makes these difficult choices to be stalkers or hawkers with a leer and a bookmark. We write because we believe in our deepest-down spirit that God has called us to keep naming the world. We write to serve a meal to the famished, to dress the wounds of the betrayed and lonely. We write to offer hope and a story to the depressed. We write to offer clear thinking in a muddled marketplace. We write in humility, in insecurity, in desperate prayer.

And when our book releases, shall we then don our best barracuda suit, polish our teeth, slick back our hair and begin the hard, shiny sell, suctioning ourselves to every unfortunate person who innocently wanders into a bookstore? Did any of us sign up for this?

Let's take a breath. We don't need to sell. We don't have to sell out or sell ourselves short, or sell our own snake oil. We need to offer. We've just spent two to three years composing, listening for God; we do indeed have something to offer. We offer our work, and, more importantly, we offer ourselves. In all of our promotion, we need to think, *how may I serve others? How may I serve my readers?* We might end up giving books away—a lot of books. We might do some speaking *gratis*. We might end up on the short end of the accounting sheet. We might end up praying with a stranger. But at the end of the day, the year, the decade, we'll count it differently:

We got to give. We got to give more than we knew we possessed. We got to be part of a global conversation. We got to know new readers, who taught us more than we knew. We got to pray for strangers who became friends.

Don't listen to "sell-a-ton-of-books" schemes when they violate who you are and what you're to be doing in this world. Go ahead and "fail" a book signing if you must. Be a real writer, without shame.

NINETY-FIVE

The Best Marketing Tool

Melissa K. Norris

Authors are constantly on the lookout for the best market-ing tips and ideas. We want to get our books in the hands of as many readers as possible. This isn't always just from the monetary end either; most authors I know truly believe in the message of their book. They believe it will help people and have a true desire to enrich the lives of their readers.

But sometimes it seems everywhere we turn, someone's spouting a new marketing trick. I can't remember how many posts and articles I've read about marketing. Some of the ideas are great, like the Hope and Trust Chronicles, a blog hop put on by some of my favorite authors.

Then there are the not so great ideas, like buying fake Twitter followers. It's not all about the numbers; it's about con-necting with people. Purchasing fake followers is a misrepresen-tation in my opinion.

The best marketing tool you have is you. The content you write and how you interact with people on your website, your social media sites, and in person is the most influential market-ing you will ever do. Because if you do this with sincerity, pas-sion, and genuine caring, your readers will talk about you.

And there is nothing that carries more weight than word of mouth. Think about it. You're trying to decide between pur-chasing two books and your best friend comes up. She points to the book in your right hand. "You have to buy this book. It's the best book I've read in years. And the author's website has these amazing behind-the-scenes looks and a free e-book you can download. I'd loan you my copy, but I already gave it to my mom, and you shouldn't wait until she's done with it. It's too good not to start today."

Which book are you going to purchase? The one with the prettier cover, or the one your friend is raving about?

Invest in your readers. They're real people and worth your very best. And if you invest in them, and don't just look at them as numbers, they'll invest in you.

And that's the best marketing tool a writer can have.

Acknowledgments

This book was created from blogs posts on the WordServe Water Cooler (www.wordservewatercooler.com) by authors from WordServe Literary. There are dozens of authors who contributed to this book, and many more we had to leave out for space considerations. Please read their bios in the back of this book and go to their websites. There are some really fantastic authors you're going to want to become familiar with.

I am grateful to the contributions of Jordyn Redwood, Alice Crider, and Keely Boeving for making the Water Cooler so successful. It's been a Writer's Digest Award Winner for several years. Because of your editorial eye and organizational ability, I can only say, "Great is your reward in heaven." Seriously, you're appreciated far more than I can possibly do in this small space. Thank you for your commitment to great writing and even greater books.

About the Contributors

Anita Agers-Brooks motivates others to dynamic break-throughs, blending mind, heart, body, and spirit as an Inspirational Business/Life Coach and International Speaker. She shares encouragement on the stage and from the page—reminding audiences, "It's never too late for a fresh start with fresh faith." Anita is also a multi-published, award-winning author. Her titles include Readers' Favorite International Book Award winner: *Getting Through What You Can't Get Over, First Hired, Last Fired — How to Become Irreplaceable in Any Job Market,* and *Death Defied-Life Defined: A Miracle Man's Memoir.* Find out more at www.anitabrooks.com.

Jennie K. Atkins is a manager of two teams of software engineers, one located stateside the other in Mumbai, India. When not at her day job she writes about individuals who discover God's healing grace while struggling to overcome the mistakes of their past. A native Ohioan, Jennie and her husband now live in a small valley east of Carson City, Nevada. They have four children and three grandchildren. Visit her at www.jennieatkins.com.

Rebecca Boschee is the author of two contemporary romances, *Mulligan Girl* and *Last Resort,* from Avalon Books. She has recently expanded her writing voice to include paranormal young adult and is working to build her niche there. Though born and raised in the Midwest, she's lived in Arizona long enough for her blood to have thinned. When not reading, writing, or spending precious time with family, Rebecca enjoys traveling, browsing bookstores and libraries, and visiting the many wonderful spas the Valley has to offer. Find out more at rebeccaboschee.com.

Jeff Calloway is a Missionary Writer devoted to spreading the good news and love of Jesus Christ. He serves as the Send City Missionary with the North American Mission Board in Cleveland, and has established church planter training schools that focus on training and coaching church planters in the Cleveland Metro area. He and his wife Julie have two daughters and three grandchildren. Find out more at www.jeffcalloway.com.

Julie Cantrell is the *New York Times* and *USA Today* bestselling author of *Into the Free*, a debut novel that earned both the Christy Award Book of the Year (2013) and the Mississippi Library Association's Fiction Award. The sequel, *When Mountains Move*, won the 2014 Carol Award for Historical Fiction. Her third novel, *The Feathered Bone*, an Okra Pick by SIBA, released January 2016, earning a starred review by Library Journal. Find out more at www.juliecrantrell.com.

Martha Carr is the author of five books and has a weekly blog on writing, thrillers and life in general. Her newest work, *The Keeper*, is the second in the Wallis Jones series. Martha has written a weekly, nationally-syndicated column on world affairs and life that has run on such political hotspots as The Moderate Voice.com and Politicus.com. Her work has run regularly in *The Washington Post*, *The New York Times*, *USA Today*, *The Wall Street Journal*, and *Newsweek*. Find out more at www.marthacarr.com.

Dianne Christner is a bestselling author who writes light-hearted Christian Fiction. After writing historical fiction for Barbour Books since 1994, she recently penned some Mennonite fiction works. Dianne resides in New River, Arizona, with her husband of forty-four years. They embrace the warm desert lifestyle and enjoy their family—two married children and five grandchildren. She's taught many Sunday School classes and led women's Bible studies. Dianne and Jim attend Desert View Bible Church. Find her at www.diannechristner.net.

Sue Detweiler is a wife, mom, radio host and pastor with more than twenty-five years of experience in marriage, ministry, and education. She is also a popular speaker who shares her heart and wisdom internationally on issues related to marriage, family, women, prayer, leadership, and ministry. Sue's first book, *9 Traits of a Life-Giving Mom,* hit No. 1 on Amazon's hot new releases for Christian women's issues. She is also the author of *9 Traits of a Life-Giving Marriage,* and the upcoming *Becoming a Powerful Woman of Prayer: How to Pray with Confidence, Boldness and Grace* (Bethany House Publishers, May 2017). For more books and resources or to schedule a speaking engagement, visit www.SueDetweiler.com or email info@suedetweiler.com.

Megan DiMaria is an author and speaker who enjoys encouraging women to embrace life's demands and delights. She is an active member of several writers groups and is the author of two women's fiction novels, *Searching for Spice* and *Out of Her Hands.* Megan is a social media pro, nonfiction writer, editor, and content creator. She has also been a radio and television reporter. Megan lives in suburban Denver and loves being a wife, mother, and Mimi. You can find her online at www.megandimaria.com.

Jan Drexler brings a unique understanding of Amish traditions and beliefs to her writing. Her ancestors were among the first Amish, Mennonite, and Brethren immigrants to Pennsylvania in the 1700s, and their experiences are the inspiration for her stories. Jan lives in the Black Hills of South Dakota with her husband of more than thirty years, where she enjoys hiking in the Hills and spending time with their four adult children and new son-in-law. Find her at www.jandrexler.com.

Jan Dunlap is the author of *Archangels Book I: Heaven's Gate,* a new Christian suspense novel that melds cutting-edge science with faith. She is also the author of *Saved by Gracie,* her best-selling humorous spiritual memoir, and the Birder Murder Mystery series. When she's not playing with fictional devices, Jan is a birdwatcher, a featured speaker, and the proud mother of five children. She welcomes visitors at jandunlap.com.

Dena Dyer is a wife, mom, speaker, author of eight books, and contributor to many more. She loves encouraging hurting, harried women to find hope and healing in the arms of Jesus...and take themselves less seriously. Her latest book is Love at *First Fight: 52 Story-Based Meditations for Married Couples* (co-written with her husband, Carey). You can find out more about Dena's writing, speaking, and mentoring at www.denadyer.com.

Leslie Leyland Fields is the award-winning author of 10 books, including her most recent, *Crossing the Waters: Following Jesus through the Storms, the Fish, the Doubt and the Seas.* She lives in Kodiak, Alaska where she works in commercial fishing with her family and runs the Harvester Island Wilderness Workshop for writers. The rest of the year she travels often to speak around the country on matters of Writing, Faith and Culture. Find her at www.leslieleylandfields.com.

Ken Gire is the author of more than 20 books, including *The Divine Embrace, Windows of the Soul, The Work of His Hands,* the *Moments with the Savior* series, and the *Reflective Living* series. His newest book, *All the Gallant Men,* co-written with Donald Stratton, releases from William Morrow in November 2016.

Michelle Griep has been writing since she first discovered blank wall space and Crayolas ... professionally, however, for the past 10 years. She resides in the frozen tundra of Minnesota, where she teaches history and writing classes for a local high school co-op. You can find her at: www.michellegriep.com, www.writerofftheleash.blogspot.com, or on Twitter, Facebook, or Pinterest.

Shelley Hendrix has authored several books and study guides, including *Why Can't We Just Get Along?*, which was featured in CALLED Magazine's Summer 2013 edition as a "Must Read!" She is also the founder of Church 4 Chicks, 2014 Kingdom Awards' Ministry of the Year honoree, and co-founder of Heart Smart –

Counseling, Coaching and Consulting with her husband (and BFF), Stephen D. Hendrix, LPC, CADC II. Together, the Hendrixes help individuals, couples, families and teams learn how to live a "heart smart life" in their relationships both inside and outside of the home. Find out more at shelleyhendrix.com.

Becky Johnson is an author and blogger along with her daughter Rachel at www.welaughwecrywecook.com. Their newest book, an enlightening and humorous journey about self-care, is titled *Nourished: A Search for Health, Happiness and a Full Night's Sleep* (January 2015, Zondervan). They also authored *We Laugh, We Cry, We Cook*, a humorous food memoir, in 2013.

Greg Johnson is the President of WordServe Literary Group (www.wordserveliterary.com) and FaithHappenings.com. He has been a literary agent for more than two decades, representing more than 2,300 books to ninety different imprints. Greg is married to Becky and together they are parents of six adult children and seven grandchildren. They make their home near Denver, Colorado. Find out more at www.faithhappenings.com.

Karen Jordan encourages others to tell the stories that matter most. As an author, speaker, writing instructor, and blogger at karenjordan.net, she focusing on topics about faith, family, and writing. Karen holds an MA in Professional and Technical Writing from the University of Arkansas at Little Rock. A native Texan, Karen and her husband, Dan, live in Hot Springs Village, Arkansas, near their children and grandchildren. Find her at www.jordankaren.com.

Kathi Lipp is a national speaker and the bestselling author of seventeen books including *Clutter Free, The Get Yourself Organized Project, The Husband Project* and *Overwhelmed* with Harvest House Publishers. She is a frequent guest on radio and TV and has been named Focus on the Family radio's "Best of Broadcast." She is the host of the popular podcast "Clutter Free Academy with Kathi Lipp." Find out more at www.kathilipp.com.

Kariss Lynch writes contemporary fiction about characters with big dreams, hearts for adventure, and enduring hope. She is the author of the Heart of the Warrior series with *Shaken, Shadowed,* and *Surrendered.* Making her home in Dallas, TX, Kariss can usually be found on coffee dates with friends, jamming to country music, or curled up reading a good book. Find her at karisslynch.com.

Erin MacPherson lives with her husband and their three adorable children in Austin, Texas. She is the author and co-author of many books, including *The Christian Mama's Guide to Having a Baby.* She was an editor and staff writer for a popular parenting and pregnancy website for years, where she spent hours each week researching pregnancy, talking to obstetricians and midwives, and giving out tips and advice to new and pregnant mamas. Visit Erin at christianmamasguide.com.

Gillian Marchenko is the author of *Still Life, A Memoir of Living Fully with Depression* (InterVarsity Press, 2016). Her first book, *Sun Shine Down* (T. S. Poetry Press) about her daughter's birth and diagnosis of Down syndrome in Eastern Europe, released in 2013. She and her husband Sergei spent four years as church planters in Kyiv, Ukraine with the Evangelical Free Church of America and they now live with their four daughters in St. Louis, Missouri. Catch up with Gillian on her author page on Facebook or at gillianmarchenko.com.

Dineen Miller is passionate about igniting the souls of others through God's Word and truth. She is a multi-published award-winning author of both fiction and nonfiction books, a speaker and a ministry leader. She is blessed every day to love her husband of 29 years, her two grown daughters and son-in-love, and two energetic furry rescues. Visit Dineen online at DineenMiller.com or SpirituallyUnequalMarriage.com.

Melissa K. Norris writes inspirational historical romance novels. A skilled artisan crafter, she creates new traditions from old-time customs for her readers. She found her own little house in the big woods, where she lives with her husband and two children in the Cascade Mountains. She writes a monthly column, Pioneering Today, for the local newspaper that bridges her love of the past with its usefulness in modern life. Her most recent book is *The Made-From-Scratch Life*. Find out more at www.melissaknorris.com.

J. Parker is the author of two books on sex in marriage, *Hot, Holy and Humorous*, and a collection of marriage stories, *Behind Closed Doors*. She writes the Hot, Holy & Humorous blog, where she uses a biblical perspective and blunt sense of humor to foster Christian sexuality in marriage. Find out more at hotholyhumorous.com.

Rachel Phifer is the author of the contemporary novel, *The Language of Sparrows*. As the daughter of missionaries, Rachel grew up in four different countries (U.S., Malawi, South Africa and Kenya) and had attended eleven schools by the time she graduated from high school. She holds a BA in English and psychology and now makes her home in Houston with her family. You can visit her website at www.rachelphifer.com or her writing blog at www.novelrenaissance.com.

Krista Phillips is the author of *Sandwich, with a Side of Romance* and *A Side of Faith*. She enjoys life with her husband and their four beautiful daughters in Tennessee. She is an advocate for congenital heart defect and organ donation awareness and blogs at www.kristaphillips.com.

Dr. Christina M. H. Powell is the author of *Questioning Your Doubts: A Harvard PhD Explores Challenges to Faith*. She is a bioresearch consultant and medical writer who conducted cancer research at the Dana-Farber Cancer Institute and Harvard Medical School. She holds a Ph.D. from Harvard University in Virology, where she studied how viruses can be used as a tool to better understand cancer. She is also an ordained minister with the Assemblies of God. Visit her website at www.christinamhpowell.com.

Rachel Randolph is the co-author of *We Laugh, We Cry, We Cook* with her mom, Becky Johnson. In 2015, the duo published a second book, *Nourished: A Search for Health, Happiness, and a Full Night's Sleep.* Married to Jared and a mother of two, Rachel blogs about nourishing our hearts, homes, relationships, hobbies, *and* kitchens at www.thenourishedmama.com.

Jordyn Redwood is a pediatric ER nurse by day, suspense novelist by night. She hosts Redwood's Medical Edge, a blog devoted to helping authors write medically accurate fiction. Her first two medical thrillers, *Proof* and *Poison*, garnered starred reviews from *Library Journal*, and were shortlisted for multiple awards. In addition to her novels, she blogs regularly at Redwood's Medical Edge and the WordServe Water Cooler. You can connect with Jordyn via Facebook, Twitter, Pinterest, her website (www.jordynredwood.com) and via e-mail at jredwood1@gmail.com.

Shellie Rushing Tomlinson is the author of five books, including her latest, a storytelling cookbook entitled *Hungry is a Mighty Fine Sauce*. She is also owner and publisher of All Things Southern (www.belleofallthingssouthern.com), and the host of a weekly radio talk show and daily radio segments by the same name. Shellie and her husband live in Louisiana.

Kimberly Vargas' debut novel, *Gumbeaux*, received a gold medal in the 2011 Readers Favorite fiction contest. Her hobbies are writing, painting, cooking, movies, creative projects, travel and reading. Find her at www.kimberlyvargasauthor.com.

Janalyn Voigt is a storyteller who brings her unique blend of adventure, romance, suspense, and whimsy to several genres. Beginning with *DawnSinger,* the *Tales of Faeraven* series carries readers into a fantasy land only imagined in dreams. *Deceptive Tide (Islands of Intrigue: San Juans)*, a romantic suspense novel, released in June 2016. Look for *Hills of Nevermore* (Montana Gold, book 1), a western historical romance, to release in 2017. Live Write Breathe (www.livewritebreathe.com), the website where Janalyn teaches other writers, was named one of the Write Life's 100 best websites for writers in 2016. Learn more about Janalyn Voigt and her books at www.janlynvoigt.com.

Bob Welch is the author of 21 books, including the Oregon Book Award nominee "American Nightingale," featured on ABC's "Good Morning America." He is a former newspaper columnist, a former adjunct professor of journalism at the University of Oregon and a current writer, speaker and workshop leader. He has twice won the National Society of Newspaper Columnist's "Best Writing" award. He is at bobwelch.net.

The Writing Sisters, Betsy Duffey and Laurie Myers, were born into a writing family, and began critiquing manuscripts at an early age for their mother, Newbery winner Betsy Byars. They went on to become authors of more than thirty-five children's novels written individually and with their mother. When their mother retired they made a decision to use their writing skills to share their faith. Their first book for adults, *The Shepherd's Song*, was published by Simon and Schuster's Howard Books. *The Lord is Their Shepherd: Praying Psalm 23 for Your Children* was released in March 2016. Find them at www.writingsisters.com.

FAITH HAPPENINGS.com

Are you a writer or speaker looking to grow your platform, reach and readership?

FaithHappenings.com can help you do just that!

FaithHappenings.com is an online Christian resource with 454 local websites serving more than 31,000 cities and towns. It offers tailored, faith-enriching content for members. Along with a few dozen other benefits, it connects people of faith to information about books, blogs, speaking events, and other resources that interest them most. As a writer or speaker, it will help you connect with people specifically interested in your genre, subject or brand! So, just what can FaithHappenings.com offer you?

On FaithHappenings.com You Can...

1. For Free... **List yourself as a speaker both locally and regionally**—increasing your visibility in multiple markets

2. For Free... **Announce your book signings** in your area

3. **List your books—both traditionally and self-published** (sent out to members who have requested to hear about new books in your genre)*

4. **Announce special e-book promotions the day they happen** (sent out to members and listed on the site daily!)*

5. **Build your blog traffic** by posting your blog into two categories, and be highlighted as a "Featured Blogger" on our Home Page*

6. **Be a highlighted "Author Interview."** FH Daily runs author interviews several times a week. Just email fhdaily@faithhappenings.com to see if you qualify.

7. **Create more awareness for your book with advertising**! An ad on the site is affordable for any author.*

8. As a free member yourself, you can **receive e-mail announcements for any book** in more than 70 genres

What are you waiting for? Get started today by signing up in your local area to become a member at www.faithhappenings.com.

A small fee applies

ABOUT THE PUBLISHER

FH Publishers is a division of FaithHappenings.com

FaithHappenings.com is the premier, first-of-its kind, online Christian resource that contains an array of valuable local and national faith-based information all in one place. Our mission is "to inform, enrich, inspire and mobilize Christians and churches while enhancing the unity of the local Christian community so they can better serve the needs of the people around them." FaithHappenings.com will be the primary i-Phone, Droid App/Site and website that people with a traditional Trinitarian theology will turn to for national and local information to impact virtually every area of life.

The vision of FaithHappenings.com is to build the vibrancy of the local church with a true "one-stop-resource" of information and events that will enrich the soul, marriage, family, and church life for people of faith. We want people to be touched by God's Kingdom, so they can touch others FOR the Kingdom.

To learn more, visit www.faithhappenings.com.

www.ingramcontent.com/pod-product-compliance
Lightning Source LLC
Chambersburg PA
CBHW031918190326
41519CB00007B/338